Cradle on the Waves

A Year of Living on Prince Edward Island

Mae Leveson

First published in Canada: January 2019
ISBN: 978-1-9995789-0-9
Text copyright ©2019 Mae Leveson

To Paul – for believing in me – and to Tracy – my kindred spirit.

CONTENTS

PROLOGUE

THE WINDS OF CHANGE

I had dreamed of living on an island – a flight of fancy that never seemed likely to turn into a reality until the day we found ourselves on the approach to the Confederation Bridge: our route onto Prince Edward Island.

Mention Prince Edward Island to anyone and it is likely they will ask, 'Wasn't that the setting for *Anne of Green Gables*?' People from across the world are familiar with the story of the little red-haired girl who came to live with the Cuthberts, in the fictional town of Avonlea, on Prince Edward Island, from the 1908 novel by the Canadian author, Lucy Maud Montgomery. Aside from that, most people I told about our proposed move didn't seem to know where Prince Edward Island is located or anything else about this smallest Canadian province.

Although I had visited Prince Edward Island on a day trip back in 2012, I couldn't claim to know much about it either. I recalled red sand beaches and lighthouses and Charlottetown, the provincial capital, where we ate their famous Cow's ice cream on the waterfront.

After five years of intense stress in a work environment, which could best be described as toxic, I was a chronic insomniac surviving on two hours of sleep a night (if I was lucky) and with such severe anxiety that I was barely functioning. I had been going to psychotherapy for more than a year and had been asked, 'How long do you think that you can keep going like this?' to which I had replied, 'I don't know.' Less than two weeks later my world crumbled around me and I left my job, not knowing at the time that I would not be returning. Health concerns forced me to resign from my job and I then spent the better part of a year in limbo – not working – still barely getting through the day.

My husband, whom I shall refer to as Mr Candytuft, was supportive throughout and has always been there for me: supporting me financially as well as emotionally meant that we had to rethink our spending and ultimately look for somewhere cheaper to live. Having rejected much of Canada as too remote or too expensive, I stumbled upon an advert for a house for rent on Prince Edward Island.

Initially, we both dismissed this as a crazy idea and continued looking for alternatives, but I was drawn back to this advert and made an initial enquiry. The place sounded ideal – cheaper, in a rural location yet still close to town and, best of all, a house and garden – we were both tired of apartment living with all of its noise and inconveniences.

Procrastination was the order of the day, and by the time we decided to make a serious enquiry and submit an application, the place had gone. Fortunately, an alternative property was becoming available, so we made a formal application, and then waited to hear whether it had been approved. We got the news that our application had been accepted but our move would be delayed by several weeks, as the home needed a complete renovation.

Once we knew we were definitely moving, the huge job of packing up our possessions could begin. We are old hands at moving, having never spent more than five years in one place, but that didn't make the process any less stressful. We spent weeks making trips to the box shop where, towards the end, I assured the woman that this was our last visit, only to return a few days later for yet more boxes. We turned our apartment into a warehouse with boxes stacked to the ceiling and, for weeks after we gave our landlord notice, we had people trooping in every week to view the apartment.

As moving day approached, the stress levels increased. Our move was 'do-it-yourself' after we obtained a moving estimate, from a removal company, which left us reeling. How could a move cost so many thousands of dollars? When the day arrived we were already exhausted after a couple of restless nights of sleeping (or trying to sleep) on a mattress on the floor. We had dismantled the beds in preparation.

Our only concession to our DIY move was that we had hired help to load and unload as we couldn't face the struggle of moving all our worldly goods from an upstairs apartment with no elevator, to our moving truck. Our rented U-Haul truck was twenty-six feet and we had also rented an auto-transporter (vehicle trailer) for our car, which we would tow behind.

Loading went smoothly – our hired help showed up on time and loaded our possessions far more efficiently than we would have done ourselves. Mr Candytuft said the load was packed so tightly that nothing would shift during transportation – always a good sign on a long-distance trip.

The 1,691 km/1,050 mile drive took us three days. We travelled across Ontario, Quebec and New Brunswick. We had two overnight stops in hotels along the route. Neither of us slept well. By day, we took turns at driving – a challenge for me as my last car was a Mini Cooper S, and here I was driving a twenty-six-foot truck with a twenty-foot trailer and handling blind spots (big) and air brakes. I was more than a little bit out of my comfort zone.

I was happier on the wide open road of the Trans-Canada Highway and much less so in traffic. At one point, in heavy traffic where cars were cutting in front of me, I announced, 'I can't do this – get me out of here!' I quickly found somewhere to pull off the road so that we could change drivers.

As we headed east, the scenery changed from wide open valleys with the Laurentian Mountains in the distance, through Quebec, to the coniferous forests and more rugged landscape of New Brunswick. The road here had wildlife fencing and frequent signs warning of the danger of moose.

There are, on average, four hundred moose-vehicle collisions a year and many fatalities (both moose and drivers). Drivers are encouraged to 'think moose' and scan the roads, especially between dusk and dawn when visibility is reduced and moose are most active. Bull moose are large, standing up to 2.1 metres/6 foot 10 inches at the shoulder and can weigh 800 kg/1,800 lbs, so are best avoided. A moose's coat is dark and their eyes don't reflect headlights, making them especially dangerous and difficult to see on the roads. For this reason, we had planned our trip so that we reached our overnight stops before dark.

Those who have never been on a long road-trip would find it hard to imagine what it is like to drive endless miles from dawn till dusk over several days: it takes its toll, even with two drivers. Sharing the driving helps and certainly, having a companion in the cab makes a difference. We once did a move to the Maritimes in separate vehicles when I drove our van and Mr Candytuft drove our moving truck – both of us having to do the entire drive – we could barely drag ourselves out of the vehicles after three days of sitting in more or less one position. On that occasion, our truck broke down in Quebec, which added six hours to the journey whilst we awaited rescue.

Fortunately, on this occasion, our journey went more or less as planned apart from a detour in Montreal when our GPS led us astray and we ended up on the north shore of the Saint Lawrence River instead of following the Quebec Autoroute 30 (southern) bypass.

The signage in Montreal is poor and exclusively in French. This, combined with heavy, fast-moving traffic, makes navigating through the city extremely challenging. We found a tourist office and they helpfully supplied us with a local map and directions to get us to a bridge at Trois-Rivières, where we were able to cross to the south side of the river and get back onto the Trans-Canada Highway. It cost us valuable time and added a bit of extra distance to our journey, but at least we were still trucking!

Our final day on the road and our journey started before dawn, as we were anxious to arrive at our destination around lunchtime and we still had six hours of driving ahead of us. We were driving from our overnight stop in Edmundston and on through New Brunswick, at dawn. We watched as the first hints of daylight appeared in the east and gradually tinged the sky pink. An eerie mist hung low in the valleys and the air was crisp and cool – so unlike the heat and humidity we had left behind us in Ontario.

We planned to stop for breakfast in Woodstock, where there is a truck stop that can accommodate large vehicles and they are open twenty-four hours. Breakfast is available at any time and there are endless cups of tea (for me) and coffee (for him). We made good time and headed to the restaurant and enjoyed our breakfast. The servers were efficient and the food arrived quickly – they know that people are on the move and need to get on with their journeys.

After breakfast, we swapped places and I took the wheel. As we were now heading due east, the sun was blinding. I was wearing sunglasses and a wide-brimmed straw hat to reduce the glare, as it was far too bright to manage without it. Mr Candytuft was playing the role of tourist, taking photos out of the window, but also sneaking in a few of me in action. He later said that we needed some photos to remember the occasion when I became a trucker, if only for a few days.

Our spirits were high on this last day on the road. We both felt a sense of relief at the fact that the long drive was almost over and we would soon be on Prince Edward Island. We left the Trans-Canada Highway just east of Moncton, New Brunswick, and turned onto the much slower Highway 15, which follows the shore to Port Elgin. At this stage, I was co-pilot, so I was able to enjoy the views. We got our first glimpses of the waters of the Northumberland Strait.

Anticipation mounted as we approached the final leg of our journey, which had taken three days and crossed three provinces. We eagerly awaited our first view of the Confederation Bridge – our route onto the island that we would soon call home and the province of our destination. We saw tantalising glimpses of the bridge in the distance, as it is elevated to allow maritime traffic to pass beneath.

The Confederation Bridge took four years to build and opened in 1997. It is 12.9 km/8 miles in length and its curved structure spans the Northumberland Strait, which separates mainland Canada (New Brunswick and Nova Scotia) from Prince Edward Island. It is the longest bridge crossing ice-covered waters (in winter) in the world and one of Canada's top engineering achievements of the twentieth century.

We headed up onto the bridge and I admired the views and took lots of photographs. The day was perfect for this first crossing, with an almost cloudless blue sky and calm conditions. The drive across took about ten minutes and as we headed off the bridge, we arrived on Prince Edward Island. Looking back, I saw the magnificent structure of the bridge behind us and ahead, a place of green rolling hills and fields of oilseed rape and potatoes, for which the Island is famous. For the first time in three days of travel, we changed direction and were now heading west across the Island.

Approaching the end of our journey and reflecting on the events of the past eighteen months, we wondered what the future might hold. For now, we were just grateful to have arrived. We were looking forward to a good night's sleep at the hotel where we had booked accommodation for the night before move-in day.

We checked in to our hotel, then headed out to sign the papers for our new home and to pick up the keys. We were anxious to go and look at the house but were informed that it wasn't quite finished yet. The workmen were still there and were likely to be working late into the evening.

The first we had heard about our new home not being completed was when we received a telephone call a few days before our move when we were asked if we were still planning to move in at the beginning of the month and whether we could delay it for a few days. Any such delay was impossible, as everything had been scheduled around a move-in date of the first of the month. Our truck was booked, as was our moving help and all of our en route accommodation.

Once we had signed the paperwork, we drove round to look at the house. Our first impressions were favourable. It stands on the edge of the community and backs onto open fields. In the distance, there is a water view, as the property overlooks a bay. There is a garden at the front with a maple tree and further garden along both sides and to the rear of the house. Steps lead up to the front door, which, at the time of our arrival, was wide open. There is also a small deck leading to the back door. The house has grey siding and white trim and doors.

There was lots of noise coming from inside and, after putting our heads around the door, we decided that retreat was the only option. We greeted the workmen but didn't enter the kitchen as it was already so crowded. How everyone was managing to accomplish their designated task was beyond me, as they were so crammed into that small space.

We headed into Summerside – designated as Prince Edward Island's second city and principal municipality for the western part of the Island – to deal with some official documentation. Each province in Canada has its own licensing for health care, vehicle registration and drivers' licences. This means it is necessary to register upon arrival in a new province to be eligible for health care coverage. In the meantime, the province of the previous residence continues to provide coverage. I had done my research and discovered that eligibility for health care coverage starts two complete months after the month of registration. By registering immediately upon arrival, which happened to be the last day of the month, we would be eligible within less than nine weeks, as opposed to waiting almost thirteen weeks if we registered the following day.

We enquired about vehicle registration requirements and were told that we had a grace period for this and for applying for Prince Edward Island drivers' licences, so there was less urgency to address these immediately upon arrival.

Once we had completed the official documentation and provided proof of residency, we were able to return to the hotel and have a good dinner and a quiet evening, followed by an early night. We were both completely exhausted and the following day was going to be a long one.

I had set the alarm for 5 a.m. because we wanted to be at the house early for two reasons. We still hadn't actually been inside further than stepping over the threshold and had little idea of the size of the rooms and we were expecting the movers to arrive by 8.30 a.m. We needed to get an idea of the layout and get the truck in position with the ramp leading onto the top of the front door steps for ease of unloading. This necessitated driving onto the lawn and narrowly avoiding the overhanging branches of the maple tree.

We opened the door to be hit by an overpowering odour of paint. I went around the house opening all of the windows, as well as both doors. Mr Candytuft ventured downstairs and came back with his shoes in his hands: it seemed that the basement floor (the source of the strong odour) was still wet. He had only discovered this after he had stood on it. I tried not to think about all of those volatile organic compounds in the atmosphere, from the epoxy paint used to paint the floor, as I hastily went round with the camera, taking photos of the empty rooms. I was most impressed by the cleanliness of our new home, which was spotless, and later found out that the property manager and a cleaner had been there late the previous evening, cleaning up after the workmen had finished.

By 6 a.m. we had started to remove items from the truck. As with all moves, it is the small stuff that takes the longest to load and unload, as it always seems to go in last. We wanted this out of the way before our moving help arrived to unload the bigger pieces of furniture and heavy boxes.

One of the problems I had encountered in planning our move was obtaining moving help on the Island. I had searched the local free ads without success; I had asked the property manager if she could recommend anyone locally and I had tried to book moving help via the same website I had used to book help in the city. I had even managed to book someone, but this person subsequently proved impossible to contact and, after waiting ten days for a response, I started to get stressed about the idea of being stranded at our destination and struggling to empty a truck-load of household possessions on our own. We had done this before (twice) and it had nearly killed us. On each occasion, we had spent two entire days unloading and neither of us could face doing it again. I finally tracked down a company offering moving help and duly cancelled the first person and booked the alternative. I got a fast response – always a positive sign – but then the guy spent five minutes on the phone telling me why he couldn't help me. When I explained about our predicament and how we had struggled before, he finally agreed to help for an additional fee. At that point, I think we would have paid whatever amount he asked for.

The issue had been the distance he had to travel to come and help us and the expense entailed in doing so. He was based in Memramcook, New Brunswick, which is 125 km/78 miles from here, with a travel time of an hour and a half. Travel via the Confederation Bridge incurs a toll fee of $46.50, which added to his expenses. He said he would leave home at 7 a.m. and we should expect him around 8.30.

Our moving help arrived on time: three French-Canadian guys who were polite, hard-working and helpful. I think that they were a little surprised that we had already started unloading, but they soon took over the job and I was only too happy to become the coordinator, as the hall echoed to the sound of 'Where would you like this?' The only issue was the queen-sized bed, which was destined to go upstairs and proved to be something of a challenge. The house certainly wasn't designed with any large pieces of furniture in mind. There is an interesting little turn near the bottom of the stairs, which are steep and narrow but, with three strong guys there to do battle with the bed, they finally managed to get the mattress and box-spring base up to the bedroom. A glider chair proved to be more of an issue, as it wouldn't fit, but we did manage to get it upstairs later after dismantling the back and carrying it up sideways!

The house was in chaos as, in addition to the three movers coming in and out, the workmen had arrived to finish some jobs from the night before and then the cable company arrived to install the internet and phone. The two technicians who arrived first were then joined by a second truck and I began to wonder what on earth they were doing by the time they had been there for more than two hours and we still didn't have our service connected. It turned out that when the house was renovated, the fibre-optic cable had been accidentally cut, so they had to do a complete reinstallation.

At one stage, there were eleven people squeezed into our tiny house! In the midst of all this chaos, a car pulled up on the driveway and a smartly dressed guy got out, wished me a good morning, and then disappeared inside. Who was this mysterious stranger? I followed him in to find out. It turned out that he was the CEO of the property management company and he had come down to personally welcome us to our new home. He explained about the lateness of getting the house finished and assured us that any outstanding jobs would be attended to in the coming days.

The movers worked so fast that they had the truck emptied and everything in its assigned spot within two hours. We couldn't believe the speed and efficiency of their labour and were very impressed. They were definitely worth their weight in gold. We waved them off before turning our attention to the task of starting to make some sort of sense of our new home.

My first priority was finding supplies for making our first cup of tea in our new home. I had a kettle, teabags and milk to hand and we made do with a couple of cups from our picnic set. We toasted our new home with our cups of tea before I stashed a bottle of fizz to chill for a proper toast later in the day.

Gradually, the workmen left and the cable company technicians completed the installation. We finally had the place to ourselves! We savoured a few minutes of quiet – we did at least have a sofa to sit on – before setting to work. We knew from past experience that assembling beds was a priority, as there is little more uncomfortable than sleeping on the floor (even if it is on a mattress). Inevitably, there was a lot of unsealing of boxes, only to discover that the contents were not what we were looking for. After weeks of packing, the labelling of boxes becomes vaguer. The worst culprit was Mr Candytuft, who sometimes failed to label boxes at all.

By mid-afternoon, we were both flagging. Our energy levels had hit rock-bottom, not helped by infrequent meals and a four-day move, after a busy final week of packing. We admitted defeat, abandoned the unpacking and headed out for a meal at the hotel where we had spent the previous night. I seriously considered ordering a pillow with my meal, as I was so tired that I could have put my head on the table for a quick nap. We had survived our third long-distance move across Canada and we could now take our time settling into our new home. For now, all that I was looking forward to was a night in my own bed and hopefully, a decent night's sleep after days on the road.

One of the first things that I noticed about our new home was how quiet it was, or rather how quiet it was outside. After living in a city where my ears had been assaulted by stimuli both day and night, the silence was deafening. As an early riser, I was up at dawn and watched the sunrise over the bay. The days were occupied with catching up with laundry, which I was able to hang to dry outdoors in the fresh air, making sense of the kitchen so that I could actually consider cooking in it and finally sharing our first home-cooked meal in more than a week.

Three days after move-in day we were both ready to escape. There is only so much unpacking you can face in one week. We headed to Charlottetown, the provincial capital of Prince Edward Island, for a few hours of rest and relaxation. We had lunch at a British pub, where I enjoyed a delicious curry and then visited the St Dunstan's Basilica, the Roman Catholic Cathedral, which was built in 1913 in the French Gothic style. We saw a sign outside inviting visitors to enter and look around and, as it was a scorching hot day, we decided to do so. Inside was cool and quiet away from the bustling tourist crowds. A leaflet provided information about the church and I learned that this was the fourth church on this site: the previous cathedral was damaged by fire. It was lovely to enjoy the peace and tranquillity of this magnificent building and to take a few minutes for quiet contemplation before rejoining the tourist crowds and heading home.

There is something about September and the subtle shift in seasons. Although the calendar indicates that autumn does not officially arrive until the equinox, the nights are already drawing in and the mornings have that crisp, fresh feeling to them. There are days when it is no longer comfortable to venture out without a light jacket and some when a pair of gloves would not be classed as being overdressed. It feels to me like a time for new beginnings, which, I suppose, stems from my early years when it marked the start of school and the end of the holidays. For this reason, I have decided to mark the start of our year on Prince Edward Island by beginning in September – a month of mists and mellow fruitfulness – to quote Keats. Consider the earlier part of this work to be the prologue and what follows, to be the start of the story.

CHAPTER ONE

SEPTEMBER: ON THE BOARDWALK

A little over two weeks have passed since our arrival on the Island and we have seen little of the place beyond the endless unpacking of boxes and occasionally coming up for air to hang some laundry on the washing line. It is time to get out and explore, so we decide on a trip into Summerside to go for a walk on the boardwalk. Instead of heading towards town, we walk in the opposite direction, which proves to be a wise choice and just what we need: fresh air and exercise, with the added bonus of a sea view.

There is something magical about boardwalks. Not only do they head in a set direction, so there is no need to think about where one is walking, but each step brings a sense of calm and an awareness of surroundings. Walking on wood brings a connection to nature and is springy and comfortable underfoot (though it is necessary to pay attention to those uneven boards, to avoid an undignified trip or fall).

We soon discover that, if you want to meet people, this is the place to be. Not only does everyone greet you with a cheery 'Good morning' but they are willing to stop and engage in conversation, should the opportunity arise. We chat to dog walkers about their dogs, nature-lovers about the birds and animals to be seen, and locals who are happy to stop and chat. A

Royal Canadian Air Force veteran tells us about his postings, both in Canada and overseas, and we chat with a woman in her sixties, who tells us she was born and raised here on Prince Edward Island and she will never live anywhere else. Mr Candytuft and I soon decide this is a favourite place to walk and become daily visitors; quickly recognising other regular walkers who, like us, don a pair of sensible shoes and head out for daily exercise. It makes a refreshing change from pounding the pavements and breathing the traffic fumes in the city, although, with a neighbouring sewage treatment plant, there are times when the air is a little less than fresh!

The walk is constantly changing due to the coastal influence of the weather. It can be hot and sunny one day and cold and slightly misty the next. The wind seems to have a strong influence on the conditions and there are times when we are grateful for the shelter of the trees. At times, the only sounds are our footsteps on the boardwalk and the calls of birds and squirrels in the trees.

The one constant is the tides, which come and go each day, twice a day. One day, the water is high onto the shore (a spring tide) and another time, the tide is out and the sandy beach exposed with a strange kind of seaweed (almost like brown/black sea grass) piled on the shore like bedding in a barn. The city is good at keeping the beach clean and relatively seaweed-free. There are tractors on the beach scooping the weed into trucks, on a regular basis.

On this first walk we spot two osprey nests perched high above us, on top of telegraph poles, out of harm's way and at a distance where the birds feel safe from predators and humans; and hear the calls of their young chicks in the nests. People stop to gaze up at the nests and watch the parents coming and going. By the end of the second week of walking the boardwalk, the parents are spending less time at the nests, choosing to perch at a distance. We speculate that they are trying to entice their broods to leave the nests but, like recalcitrant teenagers who won't get up in the morning, they show little sign of doing so, choosing to keep their heads down and call loudly for food.

Red squirrels live in the woods: at first, we think that they are shy and wary of people, but this proves not to be the case. We stop to talk to a woman who is trying to entice them out with a bag of peanuts. She is rattling the bag when a squirrel appears – it runs straight up my trouser leg. Thankfully up the outside – else I would be running around screaming – like that scene from *National Lampoon's Christmas Vacation* where the squirrel shoots out of the Christmas tree and rampages through the living room!

I am delighted to spot bird boxes all along the boardwalk and decide to return with my camera on our next visit and take photos of the different little houses. There is a multitude of different styles and colours, including a couple in Canada's colours – red and white. There are peanuts left out for the squirrels and the chipmunks and lots of birdseed, so the local wildlife is definitely well-nourished.

On another day there is an onshore wind gusting strongly. The effort walking requires forces us to lean into the wind and our progress is slow. We feel like explorers on an expedition to unknown territory. A man walking his dog asks, 'Is this the end of summer?' It certainly seems so, as the usually busy boardwalk is almost deserted: the tourists have left and there are few locals today. For a holiday Monday (Labour Day), it is strangely quiet. Labour Day is traditionally viewed as the end of summer and the return to a regular routine after the dog days of summer, and families head home before the start of the new school year. It looks like they have taken it literally and already left: even the ice-cream parlour is deserted.

The waves are white-capped and choppy. The water looks red due to the disturbance of the sandy beach. The air is salty and carries rain that, though light, is coming down horizontally and covering us in a film of water.

The roses along the shore are mostly gone now, replaced by large hips, which are effectively protected from the birds by vicious thorns. The rose bushes stand exposed to the elements and are constantly buffeted by the wind. Cow parsley, seaside goldenrod and other wildflowers that I don't recognise, bob their heads and sway about – the wind susurrates through the grasses and reeds on the shore.

There are no birds about today, so they must be keeping their heads down. We hear tweeting from the ospreys' nest but no sign of the adults or chicks. Ominous black clouds roll across the sky – even the lighthouse looks grey on this day. The tide is ebbing, not that it is obvious, as the onshore winds force the water back towards the shore.

The next morning the sun is out again, though the force of the wind is still strong. Warm, humid weather has blown in from the south and there is an onshore wind once again. With the sun's reappearance, the boardwalk is again busy with people taking their morning exercise.

As the weeks pass, we watch the changing seasons. At first, there is only a hint of the colour change to come, but a few nights of temperatures that are low enough for a frost, and the whole spectacle of autumn is unfolding. The trees are a mix of green, changing to orange, red, yellow and gold, and I'm not the only person out with a camera to capture the moment.

One quiet Sunday lunchtime finds us out for a walk and we have the boardwalk to ourselves. We spotted a swimmer in the little brook a few days earlier and have come back for another look. We pause at the bridge to watch the muskrats. These little creatures are semi-aquatic rodents that look like a beaver, but they are much smaller, with long tails acting as a rudder. There are three of them today: one on the bank eating vegetation, a second swimming about in the distance and a third on the far side under the bridge. When it spots us watching, it dives before resurfacing further downstream. We know where to watch because we have already spotted the tell-tale sign of rising bubbles. Although described as being most active at night, these muskrats seem perfectly happy going about their business in the middle of the day or, as Mr Candytuft describes it, 'Going on a muskrat ramble.'

It is some weeks later when Mr Candytuft reads an article about the Royal Canadian Mounted Police putting out a tender for 4,470 muskrat hats. It seems there is nothing better than muskrat fur for keeping officers' heads warm in winter – each muskrat hat requires two to three pelts, so 12,000 muskrat pelts would be needed to fill the order. Strangely, around this time, the muskrats disappear: could it be they are keeping their heads down?

I wake one Saturday morning and open the curtains to see the most magnificent rainbow, which extends right across the sky. The complete arc is so beautiful that it takes my breath away. I hurry downstairs to get the camera and waste no time in going outside to take some photos – still in my pyjamas! I find our neighbour, who has had the same idea, busy clicking her camera. In this part of the world, we have those big skies and wide vistas, unobstructed by high buildings. I wonder whether there really are riches to be found at the end of the rainbow – maybe we have already found them in moving here.

It is the first official day of autumn and I've been chopping vegetables for the last forty minutes. My hands are stained orange like a forty-a-day smoker: I'm chopping butternut squash. I'm making roasted butternut squash soup, which seemed like a good way to mark the change of season. The only drawback is the weather forecast for today is a high of 25°C, with high humidity. Well, we can always eat our soup outdoors. Having done the prep for the soup, I leave the vegetables coating in olive oil in the fridge.

We head into town to a craft fair. We arrive to find that the venue is busy, but instead of artisan crafters, we find mass-produced goods and a few vendors. There is one stall where the woman is selling beeswax candles and handmade soaps. I try to engage her in conversation and ask if she has beehives. I explain that we have long had an interest in learning about beekeeping and ask if they run courses. She is dismissive, stating that they are far too busy to teach, as they have another business.

The whole experience of this local event is disappointing: I know there are artisans on the Island, but maybe they have learned from past experience that attendance at such events does not generate the type of customers who are willing to pay for handmade products.

We head to the boardwalk to escape and stretch our legs, but first I have a plan to get some photos of a recently completed shawl, which I knitted. In my mind, I picture an on-location type photo-shoot with a beautiful backdrop. In reality, I am fighting the wind, with my hair in my eyes and the shawl not cooperating, but we do the best we can in the circumstances.

Once home, I finish the soup I started this morning and decide to eat it outdoors. I sit on the back deck and listen to the sounds of nature and watch the puffy white clouds drift across the sky. It is still windy, but the mercury has gone up as forecast, so it is hot in the garden.

September is the start of the apple harvesting season and we discover an apple orchard stand in the neighbouring community of Miscouche. The brightly painted yellow shed is decorated for autumn with straw bales and pumpkins, and the apples are arranged invitingly in bushel baskets, each labelled with the apple variety. We talk to the woman who runs the stand and are pleased to learn that we can get our favourite apples when they are ready in October. I love Cox's Orange Pippins and Mr Candytuft loves Russets, neither of which is common here in Canada. True perfection would be if they sold Bramley's, which are absolutely the best cooking apples, but I will have to be content with Northern Spy, which has a crisp, sweet-tart flavour and makes a good apple crumble. We learn that the orchard is open to the public for 'pick your own' and we can get a far better price for our apples if we do so: I make a note on the calendar to go back once they are in season. In the meantime, we sample an unfamiliar variety and buy Gravenstein and Paula Red, which are early season apples. I spot crab apples and think of attempting crab apple jelly, which I've never tried before. I go home and hunt for a recipe, returning some days later to buy the crab apples.

A few days later, I'm in the kitchen, where the sweet aroma of apples fills the air: that homely scent reminiscent of baked apple pie. The crab apples have been carefully prepared and left straining through a cheesecloth bag overnight, producing a ruby-red liquid, which is sour to taste. Today the process of making crab apple jelly will be completed.

The kitchen is full of steam from the water boiling in a large pan. I'm sterilising jars by boiling them, before filling them with the hot crab apple jelly. I've followed the recipe carefully and used a thermometer to check the temperature of the liquid.

Mr Candytuft wanders in and complains about the heat and humidity, asking what I am doing. I remind him that I've already told him: I'm making crab apple jelly, but he doesn't appreciate the fact that this involves generating a lot of steam. This is already a day of high humidity outdoors and I'm adding to this, but the fruit has been sitting in the fridge waiting to be used and I can delay no longer.

The canning process always seems to take far longer than anticipated: filling the jars after boiling the mixture, then boiling them for the requisite time to vacuum-seal them. I escape the heat of the kitchen with a sense of relief.

Twenty-four hours later I pick up a jar, only to discover that the crab apple jelly failed to set. I try reboiling the jelly and the addition of copious amounts of pectin but become frustrated with the whole process when I'm left with six jars of red liquid. All the recipes I read state that crab apples have high pectin content, so setting should not be an issue. Sadly, this does not prove to be the case, and I give up in frustration.

There are signs of autumn and the harvest everywhere. We pass a farm market stand on our way to Summerside where pumpkins are displayed on wagons and hay bales have been cleverly dressed up to look like people. It is drawing a lot of interest and I see people stopping to take photos. I've already taken some and shared them with my family in the UK.

Feeling somewhat 'down in the dumps' (to use one of my mother's expressions) following a stressful few weeks of moving and unpacking, I need a distraction to take my mind off everyday problems. As the weather continues fine and hot well into September, we decide to head for the beach. We have already visited a couple of the local provincial parks located on the shore, but their beaches offered limited amounts of exercise – we are both beach walkers rather than sunbathers and want to be able to walk some distance and escape any crowds. After doing some online research, I discover a beach frequented by locals, but off the beaten track and within thirty minutes' drive from home. I don't tell Mr Candytuft where we are going, but give him directions that eventually lead us to an unsurfaced dirt road – always a worrying sign of going 'off-grid' (much to his chagrin, as he is concerned about dusty paintwork!).

Anyway, the journey is worth the effort. I follow the advice and we park on a long curved stretch of road, then continue on foot. A short scramble down the sand (sadly, no steps for access, but I suppose this is part of the reason why it is not well known) and we find ourselves on a wide stretch of red sand beach, for which Prince Edward Island is famous. The land is formed from sedimentary bedrock of soft, red sandstone, which produces its rich, red soil and red sand beaches. The redness is due to the high iron oxide (rust) content.

The sand is warm beneath our feet and the grains so fine and smooth to walk on – none of that pebbly stuff found on so many beaches. We kick off our shoes and go for a paddle in the shallows and it is COLD! Absolutely freezing would possibly be a slight overstatement, but remember, this is the north shore of the Island and the deep waters of the Gulf of Saint Lawrence are coming in off the North Atlantic. I'm amazed to see some children actually swimming, as I wouldn't even consider going in any further than ankle deep.

The sun is high in the sky and the day is hot and humid, but it's too windy for my sun hat, which would not have lasted long.

The beach stretches for miles and is almost deserted aside for a few sunbathers close to the access point. We walk along and pass a couple walking in the opposite direction but, for the most part, we have the beach to ourselves. There is a backdrop of red cliffs and red sand dunes and small birds (which we fail to identify) bobbing about in the shallows. They seem to forget their ability to fly as we approach, instead choosing to run in the opposite direction. The only sounds to be heard are the cries of the seagulls and the waves lapping on the shore. We round the end of the dunes to find that the beach continues into the distance. I don't know the full distance, but believe that it extends for about five kilometres.

My mood lifts as I connect with nature and feel the sand and seawater beneath my feet. I leave the beach feeling lighter: as though a weight has been lifted from me. I'm certain that breathing all that ozone makes one feel more alive and in tune with nature.

We time our departure perfectly too. When we get into the car, raindrops are falling and the sky becomes as black as night. We make it home in time before the heavens open with a severe thunderstorm and torrential rain.

One of the features of Prince Edward Island is the ever-present wind. We have not lived here long before we discover that it is an extremely windy place. I hang my laundry out to dry and now have to take the additional precaution of extra pegs. There are days when the laundry is drying horizontally on the line; such is the strength of the wind. In many ways, this is a bonus. We get beautifully fresh air blowing in and I can air the house very quickly, which is a refreshing change from the hot, humid conditions in Ontario, but many of the locals have been warning us about the cold north wind that blows during the winter months.

Feeling fired with enthusiasm for exploring, after our trip to the beach, we pay a visit to the graveyard of St John's Anglican Church in what was once the village of St Eleanor's; before it became part of the larger community of Summerside. The church has stood on this site since 1842 and the present building is a wooden-framed structure in the Gothic Revival style. The white clapboard church has a grey shingled roof and a square bell tower, which is topped by a red steeple. It stands in the centre of the site and is surrounded on three sides by generations of past parishioners who are buried here. The church is approached from the front via a lych gate, which was a later addition, in which a plaque marks the Centennial of Confederation, which was in 1967. This year is the Sesquicentennial, which has been widely celebrated across the country as Canada's birthday.

We have passed this site going to and from town and I am curious to learn more about it. I am always fascinated by headstones and I have read that one of the Fathers of Confederation is buried here.

Amongst some of the oldest graves are those belonging to children, many of whom died in infancy. We see little Sophia who died in July 1872, aged seven months. Many of the children's graves date from around the same time and I wonder if there was some illness that caused their lives to be cut short, but there is no indication of this on the headstone inscriptions.

We discover that many of the graves belong to families who were United Empire Loyalists, who relocated to what was then known as the Colonies (and were loyal to the British Crown), during the American Revolution, which took place between 1765 and 1783.

In researching the history of this church, I discover that there has been a church on this site since 1825. The original church was destroyed by fire in 1835. To this day, many of the rural churches of Prince Edward Island are of wood construction, as there are not the funds for more elaborate buildings.

Our search for the grave of William Henry Pope takes us to the eastern side of the graveyard. A large white memorial stone marks his grave: he is buried alongside other family members. A path leads to a plaque, which was laid by the Canadian government, to mark his grave. The inscription reads:

William Henry Pope 1825-1879.
'A delegate to the Intercolonial Conferences of 1864
(Charlottetown and Québec) at which the basis was laid

for the federal union of the British North American Provinces in a new nation. This grave is marked by the Government of Canada.'

William Henry Pope was one of the Fathers of Confederation: he campaigned for Prince Edward Island to become part of the Canadian Union, which was accomplished in July 1873. Other former colonies and territories joined the Union on 1 July 1867, to form the Dominion of Canada.

I later watch a programme on television about English stately homes. The featured home on this episode is Highclere Castle in Berkshire, the real-life Downton Abbey and home of George Herbert, 8th Earl of Carnarvon and his wife, Fiona, Countess of Carnarvon.

I learn that there is a Canadian connection to Highclere Castle, through Henry Howard Molyneux Herbert, the 4th Earl of Carnarvon, who was a British politician and a leading member of the Conservative Party. During his time as Secretary of State for the Colonies, he helped Sir John A. MacDonald, Canada's first Prime Minister, to create an independent Canada. The Canadian constitution was written by Lord Carnarvon at Highclere, before being signed in the province of Prince Edward Island on 1 July 1867.

The history of Prince Edward Island goes back further than this. It was first inhabited by the Mi'kmaq, Canada's First Nation people, who have lived here for thousands of years. The Island was 'discovered' by the French explorer Jacques Cartier, in 1534. Early French settlers arrived from France in 1604 and claimed all of the Maritimes as their sovereign territory: they called the island 'Île Saint-Jean'. The British conquest of the Maritimes in 1763 led to the land becoming a British colony and being named St John Island in 1769. It was renamed 'Prince Edward' in honour of Edward, Duke of Kent, the father of Queen Victoria, in 1799, before joining the Canadian Confederation in 1873.

***

I have been on the Island for a few weeks now and I am determined to get out and meet people, so I seek out the nearest yarn shop and drive over to have a look. I meet the owner, who tells me there are drop-in knitting groups twice a week, as well as knitting classes. She assures me that the women who attend the Thursday evening class are all knitters and it is more of a social event, although there is an instructor present, should I want help with any particular project.

I decide to try the lunchtime group first, but we are experiencing a tropical storm, which is the remnant of a hurricane that devastated the communities of our southern neighbours in the United States. Winds bend the trees over and the rain comes down in torrents – the wind makes the rain blow horizontally down the street. The streets are flooded and awash with water, as the drains cannot cope with the sheer volume of this deluge. The sky is so dark that it is more like dusk than mid-afternoon. I have decided I'm not going to let a bit of rain put me off going to the knitting group, so I head out into the fray in my rain jacket, with my hood pulled up and my head down, as I can see little for the lashing rain. I arrive at the yarn shop to find I'm the only person to show up, so I stay for a while and chat with the owner, before heading home again. A brief stop in town reveals most people sheltering in doorways waiting for a lighter patch of rain before making a mad dash to their vehicles. I'm relieved to be safely home and dry once again, after a change of clothes, as my jeans are soaking wet from a dash to the car.

The following morning, the sun is out and the sky has cleared: all is right with the world. Going out to the knitting shop in that weather had been an adventure. I've already decided to try again, but this time I go to the evening group. There is a good turn-out and they are friendly, but opportunities for conversation are somewhat limited, mainly because I'm struggling with a complicated lace shawl pattern. I get some help and advice from the instructor and decide to go home and practise.

In reality, I go home, find an easier project and show up at the lunchtime group the following week. This group is largely composed of fairly new knitters. They are all friendly and welcoming and it is much more of a social gathering. I enjoy getting to know my fellow knitters over a cup of tea and vow to make this a regular session. This plan is immediately scuppered the following week because we head over to the mainland and it is impossible to fit in a trip to the knitting group in the same day.

Our plan is to go to the mainland to stock up on groceries at Costco, but first, we have to pay to leave. There is no toll collected when arriving on Prince Edward Island via the Confederation Bridge: the $46.50 toll fee is charged upon leaving and is for the round-trip. The locals refer to Prince Edward Island as 'Ransom Island': whether travelling via the bridge or the ferry, you still have to pay.

The sky is overcast and the weather is windy again. Any photos I had hoped to snap on the way over the bridge are spoiled by the blanket of low cloud and poor light. We both enjoy the bridge crossing, though the views were better last time we crossed when we were in the higher cab of the truck with a better vantage point.

We enter New Brunswick once we reach the mainland. We feel like we are on day-release, if only for a few hours. We follow the highway to the city of Moncton, New Brunswick, a distance of 140 km/87 miles that takes an hour and three quarters.

I notice the colour changes in the leaves, which are ahead of those on the Island. By the time we reach Moncton, the day has changed completely – the sun is shining and the sky is blue with puffy white clouds. People say that if you don't like the weather in the Maritimes; wait a few minutes, as it is constantly changing.

We have lunch at a truck stop on the highway. The food is surprisingly good and I enjoy a bowl of homemade turkey vegetable soup with a warm wholewheat roll. The service is fast and attentive, perhaps a little too fast, as the waitress returns to ask if we want dessert before we have even finished our main course!

As we are leaving the truck stop, we see a corner of the parking area that is cordoned off by a rope fence. It contains three carved sandpipers and a sign explains that these tiny birds stop in the area each summer before making their non-stop migratory flight of 4,300 km/2,672 miles to South America.

Our shopping trip is uneventful aside from a lot of driving around, as we don't know Moncton. Our impressions of the city are favourable: small enough not to be overwhelming and with friendly people. Everyone we talk to seems interested in making a connection and we find we are not the only ones to have moved from Ontario – some returning home after a lengthy absence for work and others who have chosen to move to the Maritimes for a slower pace of life.

We are late returning home and cross the bridge before dusk. Our final approach to the Island is in sharp contrast with our departure, for now, the sky is blue and wispy cirrus clouds are high above us. As we turn west to head towards home, the sun begins to set. The sky is streaked with orange, purple and pink and the trees and farm buildings, which are backlit as the sun sets, are silhouetted against the landscape. I am busy with our camera, taking multiple photos at every turn. At times it is frustrating, as the lens is slow to focus and I miss some of the best shots. The whole spectacle of sunset unfolds before our eyes. We see the last hints of light across the water as the sun disappears. It is the perfect end to a perfect day.

The final day of September finds us attending two community events. It is Saturday morning and our first stop is a 'book drive'. We had seen the signs a couple of days ago but failed to understand that it was actually a book sale until our neighbour mentioned she had been and had got some bargains. On heading out we follow the signs and arrive to find they are doing a brisk trade in used books. We spend about an hour browsing and come away with some reading material for the dark winter nights. Mr Candytuft is weighed down with a box of books, but I have a more modest collection of five books.

Our next stop is the multipurpose sporting and events venue in Summerside. We are attending the local dog show and arrive to find it is already packed out with visitors and dogs. The chosen hall is quite a small space for such a show, or it may be they had not anticipated such good attendance: the centre is roped off as an arena for the dogs and their handlers and there is a small seating area, but most attendees are standing and watching as the show gets underway.

Unfortunately, the room is carpeted and it isn't too long before the inevitable happens and a dog squats down to relieve itself – a cheer goes up when the owner 'stoops and scoops' amid some embarrassment. By the time this happens for the third time, there is a small cleaning squad who leap into action and clean and disinfect the carpet. The show is entertaining, but the venue is becoming hot and uncomfortable, so we do a tour of the dogs and chat to some of their handlers before heading home.

At the end of September two news reports from CBC come to my attention. The first is that the temperature on 26 September broke all records on what was officially the hottest day of the year. The temperature reached 29.4°C in Summerside, surpassing the previous record of 25.7°C, which was set in 2007.

The second report relates to population estimates released by Statistics Canada, which show that Prince Edward Island achieved its target population of 150,000. A boost in immigration, which started at the beginning of 2016, contributed to this increase. I know that moving from Ontario doesn't count as immigration, but we still added to this growth in population by arriving in the province before the end of July. With a 1.7 per cent growth from July 2016 to July 2017, Prince Edward Island is the fastest growing province in Canada, although it also has one of the smallest populations.

CHAPTER TWO

OCTOBER: AUTUMN COLOUR

The next community event I attend is the grand opening of our new library, which is known as the Inspire Learning Centre. It is a windy afternoon in early October. I arrive at a marquee that has been set up across the road from our new community library. I arrive well ahead of the start time, but the place is already busy and buzzing with conversation. I squeeze in and manage to find a seat: I sit and listen to the babble of voices of the assembled audience. I don't know anybody, so I feel like I'm here more as an observer, rather than a participant.

The marquee has windows and I am reminded of the British children's television show *Play School*, in which the presenter used to ask which was your favourite window (there was a choice of round, oval or square): an easy choice in this case, as they are all oval. They even look like the window of my childhood memory.

I am drawn from my reminiscences by the woman seated next to me, who turns and asks if I am a local. I explain that we arrived here this summer and immediately joined the library. I tell her how impressed we are with this beautiful facility and its wide selection of books, which pleases her greatly. It turns out that she and her husband are Rotarians and this new library came into existence through the vision and community involvement of the Rotary Club, to bring family literacy to the community.

I learn that the library opened its doors for the first time shortly before Christmas 2016, so it has been open less than a year. It cost $2.2 million to build with the help of funds from the provincial and federal governments, in addition to the fundraising by the Rotary Club. There are lots of speeches and I am glad of my companion next to me, who explains who is who and fills me in on local knowledge.

It is a windy afternoon and the heat of a single patio heater is inadequate to take the chill off the air. I am glad I decided to wear a coat but also relieved when the speeches and presentations draw to a close and everybody moves inside the library building. I've already used the facility a few times, so I don't stay for a tour. After attending to some library business of my own, I head home to the warmth indoors and a hot cup of tea. I'm glad that I made the effort to go and braved the event on my own (Mr Candytuft chose not to attend), as I am starting to get a feel for this community.

I am the first to admit that I'm not very outgoing and, given the choice, I prefer to stay at home in the evenings, especially once the nights are drawing in. In an effort to be more sociable, I decide to step out of my comfort zone and attend a meeting of a local branch of the Women's Institute. I make contact with them and arrange to attend one of their monthly meetings as a guest.

The first challenge is finding the venue of the meeting. The roads here are dark, with no street lighting at night, even on the highway. I set forth with my trusty GPS and drive off into the night. The journey goes smoothly and I find myself heading up the driveway of a large house, typical of the farmhouses of the area.

There is something about walking into a stranger's home that I find slightly unnerving. I try knocking on the door, but there is too much noise inside for this to be heard, so I know my only option is to walk in unannounced. I pass through an anteroom into a large farmhouse kitchen where our host for the evening is greeting arrivals. I introduce myself and I'm invited into a room beyond the kitchen where the meeting is to be held. It is already full of women and I squeeze into the middle of a three-seat sofa. The meeting gets underway and I try to actively listen in the hope of following the proceedings. There is a lengthy agenda, but first, there are introductions. I learn that I am not the only invited guest, as there are a couple of other women who are thinking of joining. We go around the room introducing ourselves and are asked to explain the origin of our names. The only thing I can come up with is that my parents liked my chosen name. I am not named after anyone in particular, as many of these women seem to be. I think that there is a tradition in this part of the world of naming children after their ancestors, whether living or deceased, so names get passed down through the family.

The meeting goes on far longer than I had anticipated and it is already late by the time we adjourn for the social part of the evening. I have been suppressing yawns for about an hour and a half, as it is already past my bedtime (I have been awake since 5 a.m.). Quite honestly, I don't know where these women get their stamina from, as almost all of them are considerably older than I am. One of the members informs me that she has been a member of this WI branch for more than sixty years! I chat politely to my neighbours until the first signs that the meeting is dispersing, when I make my thanks to our host and the chair of the meeting and head for home. I arrive shortly before 11 p.m. to be greeted with comments from Mr Candytuft of, 'Where have you been? I thought you had had an accident,' and explain that I have come straight from the meeting. I am more of a lark than an owl and, after careful consideration over a couple of weeks, I decide not to join the Women's Institute.

A few days later, I see an advert for wild blackberry canes on the local ads website. Ever since I've been in Canada, I've been mystified by the absence of blackberries, which are a common sight in the UK, where I grew up. I felt certain I would track some down once we moved to Prince Edward Island, but I was again disappointed I couldn't find any. I've dreamed of blackberry jam and fresh blackberries eaten straight from the bush. The solution seems to be to grow my own.

I contact the man who placed the ad and he confirms he still has some available. We head out to the far side of a neighbouring community of Kensington and track him down. We learn that the property is his mother's and it is the home he grew up in. We have a long and interesting chat about his life and his ancestors, who were United Empire Loyalists, who fled the United States at the time of the American Revolution and settled on Prince Edward Island. There is another British connection here, as his ancestors came from Yorkshire. Everywhere we go we find connections: there seems to be a need to find out about people and where they are from, so any purchase involves far more than an exchange of money. There is also none of the sense of urgency that is so common in the city. People have time for one another and value listening to others' stories.

It is the second Monday of October, which is the Canadian holiday of Thanksgiving. As we don't have family here and we didn't grow up celebrating Thanksgiving, this is a fairly low-key event in our household, with a special meal, but no fanfare. Instead, I use the day as an opportunity to spend time in the kitchen and bake our Christmas cake. This has become something of a ritual and I enjoy the process of preparing the fruit the evening before and leaving it soaking in brandy before mixing the cake and baking it slowly in a low oven over the course of the day. The house is filled with the aroma of warm spices and hugs me like a comforting blanket.

Another milestone is achieved during the course of this week. I undertook the 1,000-mile challenge through *Country Walking* magazine, which I heard about from my sister, and then started in January. The aim was to walk 1,000 miles during the year and I reach this total by the end of week forty-one. I think about my achievement and realise that it is equivalent to walking from Ontario to Prince Edward Island, which really puts it into perspective.

We have not lived here long before we discover the ferocity of the winds. One night, I lie awake – unsure whether I dozed off – or have been restless and tossing and turning for most of the night. The noise is incredible as 110 km/h/70 mph winds buffet around our home, which I can feel rocking on its foundations: maybe it is my imagination, but it feels like it is in need of some extra support. Although it is alarming I think that, as the house had stood here for half a century and faced whatever storms had been thrown at it, it is unlikely to blow down in one night.

The wind howls and the storm rages around us. I am glad to be indoors with heat and power and not outdoors in the midst of it. My thoughts turn to how ill-prepared we are for any type of emergency. We have no plan in place for such an event and have casually disregarded leaflets issued by the Canadian government on what they term 'emergency preparedness'. Their advice is to be prepared to take care of yourself and your family for a minimum of seventy-two hours until emergency services reach you.

I lie there mentally running through what we have and what we might need – I realise we are not as ill-prepared as I feared. We have a propane camp-stove (with propane) to heat water for tea (essential) and to cook. We also have a small portable generator so we can run lighting or an electric heater to keep at least one room in the house warm. We even have a camping lantern, though I'm less certain of the status of the batteries. I think about those emergency food kits I have seen online: maybe we should consider investing in some.

The wind continues to howl and I continue to toss and turn: I drift into a restless sleep, dreaming of community emergencies and evacuation.

In the morning, all is calm and bright. They talk of the calm after the storm and this is definitely the case. The sun is in the sky – the sky is blue and all is right with the world. We venture outdoors to find that our home has survived intact and our little corner of the world has returned to normal – we have survived another storm.

Feeling somewhat elated, we head down to the boardwalk for morning exercise. We are still out on the boardwalk most days and admiring the colours as the trees put on a final display. On the sunny days, their leaves dazzle in a myriad of colours – red, gold, yellow, orange and burgundy catch my eye, as well as the many berries in shades of red and purple. I am walking with my camera now to capture the moment. On the morning after the storm, there are lots of leaves down as a result of the strong winds and a few broken tree branches, but we are relatively unscathed.

On one such walk, we pause on a bridge to admire the scenery and receive a severe telling-off from a red squirrel, which comes right up to us to complain about the lack of peanuts (at least that is my interpretation). It sits on its hind legs making a loud chattering noise, before skittering away and leaving us with the last glimpse of a bushy tail as it disappears into the undergrowth. How could we have come out so unprepared?

My thoughts turn to spring and I get busy in the garden planting spring bulbs. There are no defined flower beds in our garden and my dreams of creating a cottage garden have been placed on hold because we arrived at the wrong time of year to start planting. In actual fact, the garden centres had little left to plant and we were informed that there would be no new plants on offer until next spring. Winter is so long here in Canada, and spring is often late to arrive, but I need some spring colour to look forward to and to know that there are bulbs growing under the snow, waiting to burst forth into bloom at the earliest opportunity.

The planting is much more of a challenge than I had anticipated, as the ground is compacted and difficult to dig. I give up after an hour of back-breaking effort and have to wait until Mr Candytuft can be persuaded to help dig holes with a spade, in order to get the rest of the bulbs planted. Work progresses much faster with two of us and we soon have them in the ground. It is perfect bulb-planting weather with a mild, sunny day. Days such as these are to be savoured so that we enjoy the last traces of warmth before the onset of winter.

Back in the kitchen and I'm baking lemon drizzle cake, which we enjoy with a cup of Yorkshire Gold tea. I treat this tea like gold-dust, as it is expensive to buy here, so we limit our consumption and appreciate it all the more.

It is mid-October when we receive a call from friends who live in Nova Scotia: they are planning a road trip and would like to come and see us at the end of the week. These are our first visitors to our new home. Frantic preparations ensue, most of which seem to involve cleaning the house from top to bottom, as it has been somewhat neglected of late due to my Christmas knitting projects. It may only be October but, as family gifts have to be sent overseas, I am already late in starting them and I have an unrealistic deadline of the last weekend of October, which I am clearly not going to achieve.

Our friends arrive in the late afternoon and we are delighted to be reunited, as we haven't seen them in more than a year. We have lots of catching up to do and spend the rest of the day chatting over numerous cups of tea before a walk on the boardwalk and then dinner. The following morning, we head into town so they can have a look around, as they are unfamiliar with this part of Prince Edward Island. They head off later, on their way to visit family in New Brunswick and Ontario, with promises to catch up again soon. It is always so lovely to share their company and we feel glad to have renewed our friendship.

Friendship takes many forms and, after attending the opening of the library, I heard about the community park, which is known locally as the Friendship Park. I decide to head out to explore one Saturday morning when Mr Candytuft is glued to the sofa watching the English Premier League. Nothing can drag him away. I drive into town and locate the park, the entrance to which is a narrow driveway hidden between two rows of trees. If I had not been made aware of the existence of this park, there would have been little likelihood of stumbling upon it accidentally.

I follow the narrow driveway to a parking area and set off up the path, passing under a welcome sign at the entrance. It is a steady climb up a gentle hill and the trees provide shelter on this blustery day. I am faced with a choice of paths, but try to stay on the main path for two reasons – the first is that I don't know the layout of the park and would prefer not to get lost – the second is because there are signs warning of coyote sightings in the park. If I stay on the main path, there are other people about and I am less likely to have any unexpected surprises. The path continues to climb for a distance before levelling out and eventually meeting the Confederation Trail. This trail is a shared walking and cycling trail. It was developed on the abandoned railway bed that crosses the Island after the railway was abandoned in 1989. The entire trail system is 470 kilometres/292 miles in length and extends from Tignish in the west to Elmira in the east.

At the edge of the park, I turn and retrace my steps down the hill. I have enjoyed my walk and discovered this is another project sponsored by the Rotary Club and established for the enjoyment of locals and visitors alike.

It is the last weekend of October and we are heading to the apple orchard. We had planned to visit around mid-October but somehow managed to leave our visit until the very last day of public picking. The first challenge is to actually find the place, which is a little off the highway. We turn down a narrow track and trundle along for a considerable distance, following apple signs. We arrive in a parking area on the edge of the orchard where many families have gathered – enjoying the apple harvest.

As first-time pickers, we go to the stand for directions. There are little red carts with bushel baskets for picking. I am disappointed to hear there are no Cox's Orange Pippins, as they have all been picked. It seems they only have four trees, so my much-anticipated taste of childhood will remain tantalisingly out of reach for another year.

We trundle along with the little cart to the area where the Russets are located. The trees are in neat rows, their yellow-gold leaves shining in the sunlight, like golden sweet wrappers in a chocolate assortment, concealing their treasures. At first, it seems like the apples within reach have all been picked, although some remain in the highest boughs, once we venture further down the row, we find trees still laden with fruit.

I remember that apples should come away easily with a gentle twist. This may be my first time picking, but I soon feel like an expert. There is a rhythm to the process and I wander happily through the branches seeking the best apples.

Once we have filled our basket, we return to the stand to ask about apples for baking. We have already discovered that no one grows Bramley apples here, so we are directed to the trees of Cortlands. The trees in this part of the orchard shimmer in cloaks of orange-gold foliage; their ruby-red fruit stands out in sharp contrast.

This time I head straight down the row of trees towards the middle and find a bountiful crop of beautiful apples. The heady smell of decaying apples is almost overpowering. Many of the trees are surrounded by windfalls that litter the ground below, and wasps are buzzing around lazily, drunk on the decaying fruit. There are so many apples that we quickly fill another bushel basket before returning to the stand with our load. We have picked about thirty pounds of apples.

As Hallowe'en is approaching, I remind Mr Candytuft that we should buy some treats. He says he would prefer to sit in the dark with the lights off and pretend not to be home, but it wouldn't be very convincing with our car parked on the driveway.

Our first visitors arrive before it is even dark. There is a ring on the doorbell followed by loud knocking. I go to the door and find two boys of about nine who stand there wordlessly holding out their bags. I wish them a 'Happy Hallowe'en' and they grunt something unintelligible. It seems they are only in it for the free chocolate. They hurry off with their loot to go and try their luck elsewhere. Over the course of the next two hours, we get a total of about twenty callers, ranging in size from the little ones who can't even reach the doorbell and are so excited to be out, to those who are taller than us and, I suspect, probably old enough to have given up asking total strangers to give them treats. Oh well, we enjoyed the excitement of the little ones and at least it was all over by 7.30.

CHAPTER THREE

NOVEMBER: MARITIME DAYS

November rolls around, bringing blustery and wet weather. It is late morning and I am sitting at my computer writing. The rain is absolutely pounding on the roof above my head and sluicing down the street. The prevailing wind is bouncing the rain off the window and low cloud obliterates the view. We are experiencing yet another burst of maritime weather. We are quickly becoming accustomed to such storms, which occur with increasing frequency.

Remembrance Day falls on a Saturday this year. The day dawns bright and sunny but cold, as the temperature is minus 3°C. We head into town to the service at the community arena. We arrive at 10.30 and find a sea of people heading towards the venue. The car park is full to overflowing and we park in a neighbouring street and walk in. Inside, we find people of all ages assembled and waiting for the ceremony to start. In the background, there is music playing and Sarah McLachlan is singing 'I Will Remember You'. There are large video screens at either end of the arena displaying poppies inscribed with 'Lest We Forget'. Images of falling poppies are screened around the boards of the ice surface. The surface itself has two walkways across it for the parade and, slightly incongruously, there are curling stones lined up on the ice because this service of remembrance is being held in the middle of The Road to the

Roar. Curlers from across Canada are participating in curling pre-trials. The 4,000+ seat arena is filled to capacity with people standing at the back.

We are seated close to the cross in a corner of the arena, and the local sea cadets form the guard of honour at each corner of the memorial. They stand with their heads bowed throughout the parade. Veterans who are not marching have front-row seats; the dignitaries assemble on a dais.

The parade begins and the flag-bearers march across the (covered) ice and take up position behind the cross. They are followed by two columns of military personnel, local emergency services and cadets.

We stand and the service begins with the singing of the national anthem, 'O Canada', and a service of prayer and reflection, which is followed by 'The Last Post' and two minutes' silence as we remember the men and women who gave their lives so that we could live in freedom and peace.

There are no survivors of the First World War still living now: the last known First World War Canadian veteran died at the age of 109 in February 2010. I think of the bloodiest battles of the First World War in which Canadian troops displayed such courage – Vimy Ridge and Passchendaele come to mind. Yesterday was the hundredth anniversary of the end of the Battle of Passchendaele, in which 16,000 Canadian troops were killed or wounded.

The Roll of Honour is read, beginning with the fallen of the First World War. In a town with a population of only 3,000 people in 1916, forty-four men lost their lives whilst serving.

The Roll continues with the fallen of the Second World War. Within four days of Britain declaring war with Germany on 3 September 1939, over two hundred men enlisted: this was before Canada declared war on 10 September. All men who were posted overseas in the early years of the war were volunteers: although conscription was introduced in 1941, young men who were called up were required to serve on home defence duties for the duration of the war. Conscripts were not ordered to serve overseas until after D-Day when there were high casualty rates amongst the infantry. The order came into effect on 22 November 1944.

As we listen to the names being read from the Roll, we hear several from the same family. There are numerous instances where families had two or more sons serving in the armed forces. The community lost many husbands, sons and brothers during the long years of war.

The laying of the wreaths follows before the closing prayer and 'God Save the Queen'. The parade marches off and the salute is taken by three of the civic dignitaries. We leave the arena and as we exit, our poppies are collected in baskets to be taken to the town's cenotaph and laid there as a sign of respect for the war dead. The assembled crowd disperses and heads home. The town is quiet and the streets deserted on this Remembrance Day where normal life has been suspended and shops will remain closed for the day.

No sooner is Remembrance Day over then it seems that Christmas is upon us. I venture into the local shopping mall the following day and hear Christmas music playing and see staff busy preparing Christmas window displays.

In our neighbourhood, I notice a house completely decorated for Christmas, yet it is only 13 November: still far too early for such adornments. Our local shop is in a building that has sprouted two angels overnight. They stand on the roof, weighted down by sandbags, lest they should take flight. I joke that the angels have landed. Whether they will still be there by 25 December remains to be seen, as this place is renowned for its windy conditions.

November is a drab month – there is no escaping the fact. The weather deteriorates and we start to suffer from cabin fever when we can't get outdoors for fresh air and exercise. A whole weekend passes during which the furthest I venture is outside the door to throw some stuff in the bin.

Trips to the supermarket become a highlight of the week because they offer an opportunity for a change of scene. Every time we venture into one of the supermarkets in town, into the local mall, or to the liquor store, we see the Salvation Army collectors with their Christmas kettles. These kettle workers or 'bell ringers' appear at various locations and they ring the bells to subtly remind people of those members of our community who are in need at Christmas. I want to donate each time I see them and I feel guilty about walking past without dropping some money into the kettle, but there is a limit to how much support I am able to offer when I'm not working.

We resort to walking on the indoor track at the arena in an effort to get some exercise. All thoughts of venturing outdoors for a walk evaporate when I discover that the outdoor temperature is around freezing, but with a wind chill of minus 7°C. Even walking the short distance to the building from our vehicle is enough to convince me that I don't want to spend time outside on such a day as this. I'm bundled up to my eyeballs with a down jacket with hood, scarf, hat and gloves and yet I can feel the biting cold of the wind stinging my face.

One mild afternoon, we venture down to the boardwalk for a walk. Mr Candytuft insists on wearing shorts, which elicit a lot of comments from fellow walkers. I'm warmly dressed in heavyweight fleecy trousers and a winter jacket, complete with hat and gloves. After weeks with no sightings, we see the muskrats at play: three of them are out enjoying the sunshine. One swims about in the stream, diving periodically, only to reappear further downstream. The other two seem to be doing a spot of grooming. It is interesting that they are in a stream where we have not seen muskrats before and we wonder if they have relocated for the winter from the more exposed stream at the shore, into this wetland area.

It is the third week of November and the morning dawns clear and bright. There is a hint of pinkish-mauve to the sky, but appearances can be deceptive. It may be sunny, but it is far from warm. The outside temperature is minus 7°C: factor in the wind chill and it feels like minus 14°C.

I spend the morning indoors, writing until I decide it is time to get some fresh air. We haven't walked outdoors for four days, preferring to exercise on the indoor track. I check the weather before I go out so I can dress appropriately. The wind chill is still minus 11°C. I bundle up in thermals, fleecy trousers, a wool sweater, hat and scarf, down jacket with hood and sheepskin gloves. I head out to walk to our mailbox.

As in many areas of Canada, our mail is not delivered to our home, but to a community mailbox. Our mailbox is located at the local shop, about ten minutes' walk from home. As soon as I get outside, the wind hits me full in the face. I have my hood up and my head down, as I battle along. The wind feels like needles stinging my exposed skin and numbing my lips. I'm determined not to be defeated, so keep walking, but take a shortcut to the shop instead of my usual route. It is a relief to finally change direction and have the wind behind me and not in my face.

I collect our mail and make the return trip, feeling a sense of relief as I reach home and step into the warmth. I may not have walked far today, but I have no intention of going back out into the wind. This is an early taste of things to come: it could be a long, cold winter.

The next day is a complete contrast. It is 6°C when we get up and I decide to take advantage of this mild weather and put laundry out to dry on the line. We head into town and go to the boardwalk.

The air is mild, though there is a hint of cold on the breeze. The first evidence of the colder nights is the slushy ice forming along the shore, where weedy conditions reduce the wave action. The ice is a strange brown colour; due to the effects of the muddy bottom. The water along this part of the harbour and close to the lighthouse is shallow: there is surface ice extending about one hundred metres offshore.

We are not the only people out enjoying the milder weather. We see family groups, dog walkers, joggers and cyclists. Crows sit high in the trees along the wooded section, caw-cawing their alarm as we approach. The stream where we watched the muskrats last week is partly frozen; an icy film forming on the water. There is no sign of the muskrats this morning.

After we finish our walk and return to our car, we are heading in the general direction of home when Mr Candytuft makes a detour and pulls up outside the fish and chip shop. It seems he has other ideas for lunch, rather than the homemade soup that I had planned. We enter the restaurant and the owner greets us as regulars (we have been in a few times since we arrived on Prince Edward Island). It may be out of season, but the restaurant is still busy and has been so almost every time we have eaten here.

We order fish and chips with pots of tea to wash them down. The food arrives – the fish in a perfectly golden, crispy batter and the chips fried to perfection. There is a daily special that includes an ice-cream sundae, but I am left wondering how anyone manages to eat one, as I am stuffed before I finish my lunch and Mr Candytuft volunteers to clear my plate.

Whilst we are finishing our lunch, the owner comes out with three ice-cream sundaes for another table, before coming over to ask us if we have room for dessert. We groan at the idea and decline, informing him that we could use a couple of pillows for a nap after such a large lunch!

We arrive home and I bring the laundry indoors from the line as the sky is darkening with menacing clouds. A few minutes later, the heavens open and the rain persists into the night.

I wake at 2.45 to the sound of wind and rain lashing the window and pounding on the roof. I lie there listening to the storm, which rages on. I'm up before dawn and, when I look out through the window, I discover that the rain has turned to snow – not the picture-postcard fluffy white variety – more of a wet slush. Winter has arrived.

Two days later and the snow has gone for now. I head out for a solitary walk along the boardwalk. Mr Candytuft is laid up with sciatica. The morning is cool and crisp, but dull, with a grey sky and grey sea. The sun comes out and the sky brightens, though grey clouds loom in the distance. I see the muskrats in their old spot in the stream.

Like me, other walkers are out enjoying their morning

exercise and dodging the rain. I finish my hour of exercise and return home before the heavens open yet again.

As November comes to a close, I am still frantically knitting a sheep scarf for my young nephew. The pattern is driving me crazy, as it is so complicated and knitting has become stressful, rather than relaxing. I take it to the knitting group to show them my progress, but don't attempt to work on it there, as I need complete concentration for this pattern.

From misty mornings to torrential rain, we have seen more than our fair share of weather in the last couple of weeks. These maritime days have been some of the wettest we've seen in a long time.

One morning in late November, we awake to see the first dusting of snow, which resembles a sprinkling of icing sugar on the top of a cake. Considering the time of year, we have been fortunate to escape the winter storms affecting the other Maritime provinces.

CHAPTER FOUR

DECEMBER: CHRISTMAS IS COMING

It is the beginning of December and we are in town buying a Christmas tree. We wouldn't normally get a tree this early, but we were talking to the seller yesterday and this sale of trees is being coordinated by the Lions Club, who are raising money to feed local families in need this Christmas.

In the past, we have always tried to buy trees to support worthy charities and this sale is also supporting the work of the Salvation Army, so we have agreed to come back and buy a tree. Mr Candytuft instructs me to go and find a tree whilst he prepares our vehicle. I talk to one of the volunteers, who helps me to select from the smaller trees, as some of them are enormous. I select what I consider to be a suitable tree, only for Mr Candytuft to show up and say, 'We can't take that one. We need one which is not opened up if we are to get it in the car.' The seller clambers through a pile of larger trees and emerges with one he says is about the same size as the one I chose. We pay and load the tree before heading home.

The fun begins once we try to get it into the house. Mr Candytuft has already trimmed off some of the lower branches to accommodate the tree in its stand. We bring it in, position it in the stand and cut it free of its bindings, only for a shower of needles to hit the floor, like dandruff.

How is it that a tree selected outdoors always looks so much bigger once inside? We have a small living room with only one space for a tree, which is right in the window. The tree is more than six feet high and its girth means it is blocking the window and half of the sofa from a view of the television. We try to get it closer to the window, but that leads to difficulty reaching to close the curtains and loose needles drop each time I do so.

Mr Candytuft becomes handy with a brush and dustpan, sweeping up each time he sees needles on the floor. The tree sits there, undecorated, for the better part of a week. I am far too busy finishing my knitted Christmas gifts to find the time to decorate the tree, which is definitely my domain.

I fill the tree stand with water on a regular basis and this takes care of the needle drop. This is a thirsty tree. It drinks about two litres of water per day, which is more than I'm consuming.

Finally, the Christmas knitting projects are completed and on their way. I breathe a huge sigh of relief. The house has been neglected during these weeks of frantic knitting – time for a proper clean-up before Christmas.

The decorating of the tree takes an entire afternoon and involves numerous trips to the basement where all of our Christmas ornaments are stored. The boxes of baubles and strings of lights are hauled upstairs and the decorating begins. Mr Candytuft has trimming of his own in mind, but this involves the secateurs. He trims underneath the tree to give a bit more space and shortens some of the branches to allow the tree to be positioned closer to the corner of the window. He then decides to help me with the tree lights after he sees me precariously balanced on the top of a ladder. The job proceeds much faster as I walk round positioning lights, and Mr Candytuft follows me with the main bundle. Once the lights are up, the floor has to be swept yet again, as Mr Candytuft dislikes needles in his socks.

The tree gradually takes shape as baubles and treasured ornaments are added. Our tree is a potted history of our lives together and of my interests, as it features miniature knitted jumpers, hats and mittens (all knitted by me in previous years), hand-sewn decorations and baking-themed additions: a mouse pastry chef and a gingerbread man with rolling pin. There is even a maritime theme, with Santa in a rowing boat laden with presents, and scaling a lighthouse ably assisted by Rudolph.

Once the tree is decorated, it is positioned in the window. Baubles hang in the windows of the living room, kitchen and dining area. Christmas candle lights stand in the windows and I am reminded of the song 'Somewhere in My Memory' from *Home Alone*. Various Christmas touches adorn the living room: a snowman with a lighted candle, poinsettia lights and Christmas mice in full chefs' whites, bought for me several Christmases ago by Mr Candytuft, who insists on calling them rats! Lighted wreaths adorn doors – front and back – and we are ready for Christmas. There is a lovely warm glow indoors and all is right with the world.

It's beginning to smell a lot like Christmas. We used to buy spiced Speculoos biscuits as an occasional treat, but have been unable to find them here on Prince Edward Island. I searched online and discovered they are traditionally eaten on St Nicholas' Day, which is 6 December. I find a recipe, which calls for Belgian-style brown sugar, and helpfully includes instructions for toasting granulated sugar in the oven to get the same caramel flavour.

I happily weigh out the sugar and follow the baking instructions, then set the oven temperature and the timer. An hour into the baking process and the kitchen smells wonderful – just as I imagine a sweet factory. I stir the sugar and set the timer again – all goes well until I check the sugar after two hours, only to discover a caramelised pool of sugar in the dish. Disaster! My attempts at salvaging it waste even more sugar.

Not wishing to be defeated, I start again the next morning and watch the sugar like a hawk. At less than two hours, I remove the sugar from the oven and decide not to risk a repeat of the previous day. I leave the sugar to cool whilst I am busy making soup for lunch. It is quite some time before I realise that, as it cooled, the sugar had set hard in the dish! Determined not to waste a second batch, I resort to kettles of boiling water to soak the outside of the dish until the sugar releases itself from the glass dish. Had I not been multi-tasking in the kitchen, I might have noticed that the recipe instructions state to transfer the sugar to a metal bowl for cooling to prevent such an occurrence. Sadly, I never do manage to produce the batch of biscuits with this brown sugar and abandon my attempts. I do eventually find another recipe some time later, which produces the flavour of the original spicy biscuits. These are a success and I will bake them again next Christmas.

***

As I want to look my best for the festive period, I've made an appointment in Charlottetown to get my hair done. We set off early, being unsure of the road conditions. We have a dusting of snow at home and anticipate a very different journey in winter. In the event, the highway is almost deserted. The trees and fields have taken on that winter look: the trees look ashen, as they have completely shut down until the spring. The frost-hardened fields are tinged with icy snow patches after a day of wet snow yesterday, followed by a cold night. Horses wearing rugs are grazing in their paddocks and cattle stand around their field troughs chewing the cud, their warm breath steaming in the cold air.

The highway is clear and we arrive early, so have time for a bit of shopping. The shops are quiet at this early point in the week, but will doubtless be busy later in the day and at the weekend. I go to the hair salon and chat to my stylist about the last cut. We are still getting to know one another, as this is only my second visit, but she seems to understand my hair, which is why I willingly travel for an appointment. This time I leave with a shorter, more shaped cut at the back and longer towards the front: it is chic and stylish. I only wish she could do it on a daily basis so it would always look this good. I suggest it, but she just laughs.

Back in the kitchen and I'm making Christmas puddings. I

normally make them on Stir-up Sunday, which is the last Sunday before Advent: a time when they are traditionally made in the UK. I am late this year due to being unable to obtain all of the ingredients. I had to order Atora vegetable suet online and wait for it to arrive. Mr Candytuft was adamant there should be no substitutions.

As I mix the ingredients, I savour the aroma of Christmas – mixed spice and citrus combine and surround me as I bake. The pudding mixes well and is soon packed into two pudding basins and cooked in the slow cooker. Once cooked, they are stored until required – the first to be enjoyed after our Christmas dinner – the second will be saved until New Year.

A mild day provides an opportunity for a solitary walk on the boardwalk. Mr Candytuft is at home resting as he has foot problems. I enjoy the exercise and fresh air and I'm greeted by other regular walkers who are out enjoying the day. The sun is shining and all is right with the world. Even the muskrats seem to be enjoying the weather, as they are playing in the stream.

***

Finding Meyer lemons for sale in the supermarket is my cue to make a batch of lemon curd for Christmas. I prepare the fruit – washing the skins before collecting some lemon zest, then squeezing out their juice. Lemon curd is easy to make, providing that attention is paid not to boil the egg mixture, or else the eggs will scramble. Once everything is mixed and thickened, I pour it into hot jars and leave it to cool. I'm unable to resist and taste the remaining lemon curd from the pan. The taste transports me back to childhood when my mum used to put lemon curd on my toast – a taste I will never forget.

***

It is the second week of December and we have an unexpectedly mild day with the temperature reaching 8°C. We decide to go for a walk and try to get out before the forecasted rain arrives. Twenty minutes into our walk, the heavens open. I offer to head back to the car to pick up Mr Candytuft, as I'm a faster walker. Rain is running off my hood and into my hair, down my jacket and trousers. By the time I reach the car, I resemble a drowned rat!

A day later, the sudden arrival of severe cold weather takes us by surprise. We wake to a morning temperature of minus 11°C, but it feels like minus 21°C with the wind chill. I venture out to the indoor track, which has become a popular spot for walking: so many of the regular walkers from the boardwalk are now choosing to walk here. The car starts on the first attempt, but the engine sounds rough as it turns over and has to run in the cold conditions. I'm halfway to town before any slight warmth starts to come out of the heater. In severe cold weather, car engines have to work hard, especially when cars are not garaged out of the wind. There is a risk that the battery will go flat when a car sits for a few days and we have to add gas-line antifreeze to the fuel tank to prevent the fuel freezing.

Hurrying across the car park to the arena, I have my hood up and my head down. The wind stings my face and my legs are tingling with the cold. On days like these, it is not easy to make the effort to exercise, even if it is indoors.

The three-lane walking track at the arena is now a Mecca for walkers and runners alike. The ice pad has staged seating around it and the track is above this. Two lanes are designated for walkers and a third lane is for runners. Signs indicate the direction of travel for each lane – runners travel in the opposite direction to walkers to avoid any collisions.

The track is busy and walking involves quite a lot of dodging around the slower walkers and lapping a few of them. Walkers range in age and ability from young mothers with their toddlers in strollers to seniors, some of whom are walking with aids. My attention is drawn to the ice pad, where a little boy of about two or three years of age is learning to skate. He is wearing a helmet and is being encouraged by his mother, as he struggles to find his footing on skates.

Any plans for further trips outdoors are abandoned once I return home. I had considered going to the library at lunchtime for an afternoon of Christmas music to get into the spirit of the season, but it takes me so long to get warm after I return home that I don't want to go out again. Plans for outdoor carol singing in the neighbourhood have been cancelled due to the severe cold. The forecast is for the severe cold weather to continue throughout the coming week.

A third consecutive cold day finds me back at the walking track. It is a Saturday morning and Mr Candytuft has decided to accompany me but spends his time watching junior hockey whilst I do laps of the circuit for an hour. The players are mixed teams of boys and girls of about six or seven years of age. It is difficult to tell, as they wear so much kit that they resemble miniature Michelin men. The ice pad is divided in half, with two games in progress – one on each half. Mini goal nets are at either end and mini keepers wear helmets with face protection: all players wear helmets.

Mr Candytuft tells me afterwards that there are some good players and that, even at this young age, it is possible to see their potential as they have the determination to chase the puck and score goals. They fall over a lot but remain enthusiastic and some of the best skaters are the girls, whose technique is smoother. To be honest, I hadn't even realised some of the players were girls, but I wasn't paying much attention to the proceedings.

Children in Canada grow up learning to skate from a young age, starting when they are barely big enough for skates and using frames on the ice, which resemble Zimmer frames, for balance.

With only a week until Christmas Eve, I'm busy in the kitchen, trying to get ahead with some Christmas baking. My first job is putting a layer of marzipan onto our Christmas cake. I am determined that this year, I won't be icing our cake on Christmas Eve, Christmas Day or, like one year, Boxing Day. I pencilled a reminder on the calendar and plan to ice it on the 21st. I want to give the marzipan a few days to set on the cake and the surface to dry out a little so I don't have almond oil seeping through the snowy white Royal icing.

I apply the marzipan with a 'glue' of melted apricot jam, dabbing it onto the cake with a pastry brush. It is quite a satisfying process. Once completed, I put the cake back in its box and turn my attention to making pastry.

I'm not a pastry chef – I can make it, but I always seem to struggle when it comes to rolling it out, so I'm glad I'm attempting nothing more ambitious than mince pies. I mix the dough, chill it in the fridge, then roll out the pastry and cut circles of the pie cases and star shapes for the tops. I spoon mincemeat into the cases, top with the stars and bake them in the oven. As soon as they are done, I place them on a cooling rack and make a second batch. Two dozen mince pies are lined up on the cooling rack and the kitchen smells like Christmas.

I make a cup of tea – Mr Candytuft says he only wants one mince pie, which I duly present to him on a plate, only for him to eat two more. I whisk most of them off the rack and place them in a box for the freezer before he can demolish the lot. I want to save some for Christmas.

We make another journey to Charlottetown, this time to buy our Christmas groceries. It is another cold day, with lowering grey clouds. The sun peeps through the haze momentarily before disappearing behind a bank of cloud. The sky to the south is clear and blue, but we are heading east.

The highway is wet after yesterday's snow, but it has been ploughed. The side-roads are not in good shape, as they are slushy and very slippery. The car is soon filthy from the spray coming off the road: the windows are covered in grime and we need the wipers on to see out. Weather conditions are milder than they have been. It is good to get out after a week of sub-zero temperatures, though the wind still has a bite to it.

The supermarkets in Charlottetown are quieter than expected and we manage to shop without the usual Christmas crowds. It is a different story at the superstore, where the car park is jammed and the shop is really busy. It seems like half of the city is here. I hate crowds and can't get out of there fast enough. After trudging across the slushy car park in the wind, I feel half-frozen and opt to wait in the car at our final destination before we return home.

The drive back is sunny, but still cold. Arriving home, we discover that the wind has turned our drive into a skating rink, as the residual snow has glazed over. It is difficult to stand up, let alone unpack groceries from the car. It is so windy that I am doing battle with the doors, trying to open them. I drop my glove, which promptly blows straight under the car. Mr Candytuft moves the car so I can retrieve it, but my glove has blown to the far side of the drive. I go to retrieve it and almost fall, as I slip on the ice.

I am relieved to finally be indoors and home. In our absence, a snow fence has been erected beyond the end of our back garden. This seems like an ominous warning of the winter weather to come.

Another sign of winter is the sudden appearance of metal rods marking the edge of the road (for the snowploughs) and high flags attached to the above-ground fire hydrants. Our hydrants are similar to those seen in the United States, but they can be difficult to find in the event of a big winter storm, or even after weeks of snow accumulation.

This evening, the community carol singing goes ahead in spite of the cold. Canadians are a hardy bunch! Nothing would entice me to go back outside after spending hours thawing out after our shopping trip.

The winter solstice arrives and with it, the hope of lengthening days to come. I ice our Christmas cake and decorate it playfully with Santas in various poses, a few reindeer and a Merry Christmas sign for good measure. This Christmas feels like one to celebrate and the dancing Santas set the right tone.

I spend the following morning in the kitchen baking cookies. I make cranberry and white chocolate and a batch of chocolate shortbread to give to the maintenance crew who look after our home, as well as dropping some off at the management office. They are such a great team and are always so helpful that I think it is nice to show our appreciation of their efforts. We go over to the management office, where our cookies are well received. They promise to deliver some to the maintenance crew, who are strangely elusive on a day when I'm actually trying to track them down. Now the colder weather is here, I don't see them out and about as much as I did during the warmer months.

Three days later, the morning of Christmas Eve finds us walking along the harbour front. It is the first time it has been mild enough for outdoor exercise in almost two weeks. The consistently sub-zero temperatures have resulted in the harbour freezing over. Unlike a pond that freezes, the harbour looks like the waves just stopped moving: undulations of ice with larger chunks in places stretch as far as the eye can see. I'm not sure if they are the result of expansion as the ice formed, or if they were pushed inshore from further out in the Northumberland Strait.

There is an eerie silence with not much movement and few walkers. It is so quiet this morning that we spot two red foxes on the path ahead of us: they pause and look in our direction before they disappear into the undergrowth; the white tips of their tails visible to the last. As we approach the area where they crossed, we hear a call and spot one of them perched on a rock by the shore. It watches us for a moment, unafraid, before hopping off the rock and disappearing.

The sun is shining and the sky is blue this morning, with cirrus clouds high above us. The wind is still cold and I am glad of my hat and hood. Mr Candytuft forgot his hat, so he asks me to unfasten the hood of his jacket, which fits into the collar. He wears this yellow hood and I call him my canary. My legs are tingling with the cold and my knees are going numb, as it feels like the wind is blowing straight through my fleece walking trousers.

Although the path has been cleared of snow and treated with salt, care is needed, as some icy patches remain. At times, it is necessary to walk like a penguin – flat-footed and with feet turned out – to avoid slipping. A red squirrel runs up to us when we pause to adjust clothing, but we don't have any peanuts and it skitters off into the bush.

We enjoy the exercise, sunshine and fresh air, but it is a relief to return to the car and get warm. It is hard to believe that bad weather is on the way, but there is a winter storm watch in effect and snow is expected to arrive tomorrow.

After lunch, I listen to *A Festival of Nine Lessons and Carols* from King's College, Cambridge. For me, this signals the start of Christmas. Later, I curl up with some mince pies and a cup of tea and watch a film whilst Mr Candytuft naps. As dusk falls, I switch on all of the Christmas candle lights in the windows, as well as the Christmas tree lights and enjoy their glow in the darkness.

We go to bed on Christmas Eve with dire warnings of a winter storm ringing in our ears, but awake to find that it hasn't snowed. The weather on Christmas morning is milder than of late but still cold. We open our gifts and have a leisurely breakfast before the lunch preparations begin. There are telephone calls to family in the UK to make, and we receive calls from friends in various parts of the country wishing us a Merry Christmas.

The snow starts late-morning, as our neighbours, who drop by to wish us the compliments of the season, are leaving to drive to Charlottetown airport to meet their son. At first, there are only a few flakes falling, but this rapidly changes to a heavy, grainy powder. Within an hour, it is accumulating on the road and visibility is severely reduced: I can't see beyond the end of our street, which is a distance of about a hundred metres.

We sit down to Christmas lunch and watch the falling snow. We wonder if our neighbours will have difficulty driving home if the highway is snow-covered. Thankfully, the storm is short-lived and we get far less snow than forecast. The main problem here is blowing snow, due to our exposed location close to the Gulf of the Saint Lawrence, and to the flat terrain. Relatively small amounts of snow can quickly accumulate on exposed roads, making driving conditions challenging at times.

Our neighbours have made it safely home from the airport and all is well. Night draws in early, due to the weather, and we look out into the darkness and the twinkling lights of distant homes.

On Boxing Day, after the indulgence of Christmas Day, I feel sufficiently guilty to go to the arena to use the walking track. The drive there is rather slippery. Although the roads have been ploughed, the wind is whipping up the snow from the fields and blowing it across the roads, where it is starting to accumulate once again. The traffic is turning it into slushy 'pebbles', so it is a bit like trying to drive on ball-bearings. I navigate my way safely to my destination, but I'm relieved to park the car and get out.

The arena doesn't open until noon and I'm heading in the door shortly afterwards. The first half-hour is fairly quiet, with few walkers and runners about, but the track starts to get busy after this. It seems I'm not the only one feeling in need of some post-Christmas exercise.

Returning home is even more challenging than the drive there. The wind has strengthened and there is a further accumulation of blowing snow. On the quieter roads, such as the route into our neighbourhood, there is snow eddying in the fields and swirling across the roads, severely reducing visibility and making the roads icy. The exposed corners are particularly challenging, as the snow is forming drifts. At the final corner before home the car skids, but I manage to maintain my course and use just enough acceleration to manoeuvre out of the corner and up the slight gradient, without losing traction.

I arrive home to find that the drive has become even snowier in my absence. After spending several minutes alone outside shovelling, I go indoors to request Mr Candytuft's help. I change into more suitable outdoor gear – waterproof over-trousers and jacket – though, in reality, my trousers are already damp from tramping about in the snow.

Between the two of us, we clear the front steps and path, the rear deck to the back door and the snow on the drive. It is a relief to finish the job and retire indoors out of the cold.

Cold takes on a whole new meaning the day after Boxing Day. I open the curtains to find a winter dawn of distant clouds on the horizon, tinged pinkish-purple and with a blue-black haze. By now, there is no need for binoculars to tell that the bay is frozen, as it is snow-covered and white. The pine trees in the garden are rocking in the wind, which is gusting strongly.

The street at the front of our home is deserted. I don't even see the usual dog walkers and no one is venturing out on foot. The temperature is minus 18°C, but the strong, gusting winds result in a wind chill of minus 28°C. Imagine standing in a domestic freezer with a huge fan blasting cold air at you and you have some idea of what this feels like.

Not to be deterred, I decide to escape the domestic drudgery (the laundry) and go to the track. Mr Candytuft decides he is not walking today, but offers to drive me – an offer I willingly accept. If he drives, he will drop me close to the arena entrance and I won't have to park the car and walk.

As we step outside, the cold takes our breath away. Mr Candytuft has already started the car to allow it to 'warm up'. It started, but I wouldn't go so far as to describe it as warm.

I can barely stand up once I step away from the shelter of the house. The wind is so strong that it almost blows me off my feet, and the cold air hitting exposed skin (my face is the only bit not covered) not only takes my breath away but sends messages to my brain to get out of here. I battle with the car door, as the wind is trying to blow it closed, and almost throw myself into the car, slamming the door behind me.

We reach the arena and Mr Candytuft drops me off. I struggle to the door, head down and holding a scarf over my face. Once I reach the entrance, I have to do battle again, trying to open the outward-opening door, which is being held closed by the wind. Later, I have the same problem when I try to leave the building, as the full force of the wind is pinning the door closed. I have to lean on it with my full body weight in order to get it open sufficiently to squeeze out and hurry over to the area where Mr Candytuft is waiting to pick me up.

We are both shocked by the cold. Winters in Canada can have periods of extreme cold and we survived an Ontario winter a few years back where the temperature did not rise above minus 18°C for six weeks and the wind chills hit minus 38°C. But memory is a strange thing: we remember experiencing severe cold in the past, but we forget quite what it feels like to be outdoors in extreme temperatures. Venturing outdoors on a day like this is a stark reminder of how cold it can be and of the importance of adequate clothing (including a face covering or scarf), to protect exposed skin.

Wind chill is defined as what the temperature feels like when low temperatures are combined with high winds: loss of body heat increases with a rise in wind speed. Wind chill is how cold it feels as the body cools and causes skin temperature to drop. The combination of cold temperatures and high winds can lead to frostbite and hypothermia. Exposed skin will freeze in thirty minutes in a wind chill of minus 18°C.

It is two days after Boxing Day and this is starting to feel like the weather almanac, but the temperature this morning is minus 19°C and the wind chill is minus 30 C. It is easy to develop cabin fever from spending too much time indoors, but any motivation to be outside has disappeared as the temperatures have fallen.

The following morning, we make the effort to get out for some fresh air and a change of scene. We are on our way through town, to the library, and make a detour down to the harbour, which is completely frozen. We spot an ice-breaker clearing the channel and drive round to the wharf area for a closer look.

The freighter, *MV Shoveler*, is requiring assistance to leave the ice-bound harbour. We are not alone in stopping to see the action, as the car park adjacent to the port quickly fills up with passers-by, who have stopped to see the show. The Canadian Coast Guard vessel, *Sir William Alexander*, is on ice-breaking duty. Painted in red and white, it stands out in an otherwise drab, winter landscape. Upon closer inspection, we see that it is covered in ice at the bow and is equipped with a helicopter, which is concealed under a cover on the aft deck. We watch as they come alongside the *Shoveler* before turning towards it moving slowly and clearing the channel.

The vessel works its way around the docked freighter, *MV Shoveler*, clearing the ice. The gulls are circling and heading towards the newly cleared channel. We take it in turns to get out and take photos. It is snowy underfoot and there is a biting wind. It is not pleasant being outside for more than a couple of minutes in the wind chill. Eventually, we decide we have watched for long enough as we are getting cold, and head towards home. Mr Candytuft tracks the vessels online after they leave port: they head out of the Northumberland Strait and the *Shoveler* passes under the Confederation Bridge to open water.

***

It is the day before New Year's Eve and we are travelling down the highway. The sky is blue and it feels like the first time that we have seen the sun in weeks. We are on our way to Cavendish – a place of pilgrimage for millions of fans of Lucy Maud Montgomery – the fictional home of *Anne of Green Gables*, the strong-willed, red-haired orphan girl who comes to live here with Aunt Marilla. She may be a fictional character, but she has been a part of people's childhoods for generations. This house attracts hundreds of thousands of visitors each year. But this is a snowy day in late December and we don't expect to be meeting any tourists.

We have been on the Island for five months now and I have wanted to visit since before we arrived. I had hoped to have a chance to visit in October, before the house closed for the season, but we didn't make it. So now, I'm curious to see the house in winter. When the morning dawned bright and sunny, but still cold, it seemed a good opportunity to go out and do some sightseeing and I suggested that we head to Cavendish and visit Green Gables Heritage Place.

On leaving the main highway we head towards the north shore. The roads, which had been relatively clear of snow to this point, are ice-covered and slippery, with snowy patches where blowing snow has come off the fields. The thought goes through my head that, if this were England, traffic would not be moving, but this is Canada and life continues as usual. Mr Candytuft is driving today, though I've done my share of driving in such conditions. Thank goodness for winter tyres!

We miss the turning for Green Gables, which is situated in the national park. Road conditions are so slippery that we don't attempt to turn around and retrace our tracks, preferring the safer option of continuing to the neighbouring community of North Rustico, which we decide to explore before retracing our steps.

At the harbour in North Rustico we find all of the boats hauled out for winter. The bay is frozen and snow-covered. Behind the fish market, close to the dock, there is a row of brightly coloured fishermen's huts with neatly stacked lobster pots. One hut has a shingled roof and a bright red door and is decorated with the Maple Leaf and a collection of fishing buoys in a multitude of colours.

On our way back through town, I spot a family restaurant, which is open, and we stop for lunch. Finding anywhere to eat out of season can be a challenge once you are away from the more populous areas, so I'm glad we found this. The lunch is delicious – all the more so due to the continuing cold weather – today is a balmy minus 11°C with a wind chill of minus 19°C. Mr Candytuft enjoys fish and chips and I have a tasty bowl of homemade turkey and vegetable soup – perfect for a cold winter's day.

We arrive at the park and Mr Candytuft opts to wait in the warm car. I bundle up and head along the driveway on foot. There is a sign marked 'Authorized personnel only', but the park website states that it is open year-round. I walk up the snow-covered drive between the trees. I don't actually know if I'm heading in the right direction, as this is the first time I have visited, but it seems like the logical direction.

I pass a couple of barns and see through a gap between them. There was one other car parked when we arrived and there is a woman in the farmyard taking photos. I give her a friendly wave and she waves back. I almost keep walking but realise the house must be on the other side of the barn, so head through the gap. We greet one another and she comments on it being a beautiful day, with which I agree. It seems she is leaving, so I have Green Gables to myself.

I think of the crowds of tourists who descend on this site throughout the season and how fortunate I am to be able to enjoy my visit in peace and solitude. I am at the rear of the white clapboard house with green roof, trim and shutters. I head along the side of the house, off the path, and across the snow. The walk isn't too difficult as someone has been here before me so I can follow in their footsteps.

I round the corner of the house and find the front door, from which the land slopes gently downhill to a stream at the bottom. I descend cautiously. There appear to be steps beneath the snow, but it is difficult to feel their edges and I don't want to lose my footing and fall. At the bottom of the slope, there is a bridge leading to the Haunted Wood Trail. As I am alone, I don't intend following the walk through the trees – not because I'm afraid, but because it is very cold and I don't want to be outside for too long.

I walk onto the snow-covered footbridge with its rustic post and beam fence topped with an icing of snow, and I glance down at the frozen stream below. Bright red berries stand out in striking contrast against bare winter shrubs. There is absolute silence in this winter landscape.

I head back up the hill and take some photos before investigating another trail. The Balsam Hollow Trail heads past the back of the house and through the trees to Lovers' Lane, but I don't plan to walk it today.

Looking at the Parks Canada website later, I see this trail

leads to a boardwalk and is actually less than a kilometre in length. Whenever I spot signs for trails, I always expect them to be longer, but I imagine that the majority of tourists who visit are not interested in going for a hike.

I pass trees dusted with powdered snow and a picnic area where the benches are frosted in white. I pause to take a photo looking back towards the house. I capture a snowy scene of long shadows cast by the trees with the sun low in the sky at this time of year.

The wind shakes the tree branches and large flakes of snow come down. I pull my hood up to protect my face from the wind and decide it is time to head back to the car. My hands are numb and tingling from removing my gloves to take photos and I don't wish to risk frostbite.

My last view of the house through the trees is of pristine white snow with a single trail of footprints. The white house stands out with its green gables and green picket fence against a backdrop of greyish-brown trees, which are stark and bare at this time of year. The brilliant blue sky stands in sharp contrast with only a few wispy clouds.

I walk past the brown barns with their orange-red doors and back to the warmth of our car. We head home with the heater going full-blast and The Milk Carton Kids singing 'Whisper in Her Ear', playing on the stereo.

Any plans to go out on New Year's Eve are abandoned due to the return of extremely cold conditions after a brief respite from the severe wind chills. Canada seems to be in the grip of Arctic weather from coast to coast. The media describe the weather as frigid. Although it is not unusual to experience a cold snap around New Year, what makes this one different is the fact that it is so expansive and how long it will continue. The blanket of Arctic air is coming from Siberia and the forecast is for it to remain well into January.

Outdoor New Year's Eve celebrations across Atlantic Canada are cancelled after the temperature plummets to a low of minus 27°C with wind chill and winds gusting up to 50 km/h /30 mph causing a bitter cold.

After waking to these temperatures, neither of us has any desire to venture outdoors. We spend the day quietly at home and watch the New Year's Eve fireworks from London. Home seems like the best place to be tonight.

CHAPTER FIVE

JANUARY: SHADES OF WINTER

New Year's Day dawns with a winter sky of bright blue, but continuing cold temperatures. As today is a holiday, there is nowhere to go and it is far too cold to spend time outdoors. We cook our New Year's Day lunch and raise a glass to a Happy New Year.

After lunch, I call my mum and chat with her for an hour, then call my sister. It is at times like these that I need family contact and mine are thousands of miles away on the other side of the ocean. I spend some time filling in important dates on our 2018 calendar and wondering what this New Year has in store for us.

I am back at the track on the day after New Year and it is packed with walkers. Many people seem to have made New Year's resolutions to get more exercise. I wonder how long they will continue.

Meanwhile, down at the harbour, a temporary village of ice fishing huts has sprung up. There is a long tradition of ice fishing in Canada. The fishermen drill a hole in the ice and then assemble their tiny wooden shacks, where they sit, out of the elements, to fish for smelt: tiny fish that come in with the tide. Each fisherman is allowed to catch up to sixty smelts per day. The ice in this part of the harbour is about 20 centimetres/8 inches) thick and the ice fishing season lasts from mid-December until early March, when the ice starts to melt.

Canadians like to make the most of winter and another common sight is the homemade ice rink. We pass one on our way into town. It has been built in front of a house, which is adjacent to the highway, so I can monitor its progress. Once the weather is consistently below around minus 6°C, it is cold enough to build a rink. This one has boards around the edges and the chap has spent a lot of time grooming the ice. The next time we pass, on our way back from town, the rink is packed with young boys and a couple of parents, playing hockey. Christmas is over now and school starts again this week, so this is likely to be the last chance for weekday hockey games.

I've noticed many Canadians buy their Christmas trees and decorate for Christmas by mid-November, only to take everything down by the day after Boxing Day. As I prefer to keep to a more traditionally English schedule, our tree remains in place until after New Year.

I take our Christmas tree down and spend a long time carefully wrapping all of the ornaments and storing them in the basement. It is a couple of days before Twelfth Night, but I want to get the tree out before the forecasted winter storm. I have no desire to be doing battle with it in the middle of a blizzard.

We have our first day of milder weather since before Christmas and take advantage of it by heading to the harbour front for a walk. The harbour is frozen solid, but the ice has smoothed out since our last walk here on Christmas Eve. The large ice ridges have disappeared, presumably due to the action of the tides.

Lots of locals are out walking – some with their dogs – enjoying the milder weather before the storm arrives. Winter in Canada can be long and harsh and it is all too easy to spend all of your time indoors, never getting a breath of fresh air.

The sky is overcast and cloudy: the light is poor, but I have the camera with me and take some photos of the harbour. The path is fairly clear of snow and we are able to walk at a moderate pace. It is great to be outdoors enjoying some fresh air and exercise. We complete our walk and head into town to buy a few groceries. Many Islanders are out stocking up on essential supplies, such as milk and bread, before the storm hits.

For days now, the weather forecasts have been predicting a massive winter storm heading towards the Maritimes. This will be the first Nor'easter of the season. This is the term used to describe storms that mainly affect the North-Eastern United States. These storms form along the East Coast as warm air from the Atlantic Ocean clashes with Arctic cold to the north and west. This storm is described as a 'weather bomb', which is caused by a fast drop in barometric pressure – typically a fall of 24 millibars in twenty-four hours – in this case, the coming storm results in a drop of 35 millibars in twelve hours overnight.

The snow begins around lunchtime with only a few flakes at first, but becoming rapidly heavier and reducing visibility within less than an hour. We watch as the snow starts to accumulate and workers from local businesses head home early. Schools are already closed for the day; with the children enjoying an extra day off, having only returned from their Christmas break this week.

Large, wet flakes rapidly accumulate on the road, where cars leave tracks in the snow. A knock at the back door, which I answer, results in a face full of wet snow as soon as I open it. The maintenance crew are out collecting Christmas trees before the strong winds arrive, as gusts of 80 to 100 km/h /50 to 60 mph are forecast. We gladly agree to them taking our tree away before we have to chase it down the street.

Four hours after the snow starts, it is coming down horizontally in the strengthening winds. It is difficult to monitor what is happening outside, as the windows are now completely covered in wet snow.

From the news, we learn that the eye of the storm has tracked up the East Coast of the United States towards Nova Scotia, New Brunswick and Prince Edward Island. It has caused major disruption, with the cancellation of all flights and ferries, as the leading edge of the storm reached the shore of Nova Scotia.

As an early dusk becomes night, I hear sounds like rain hitting the windows. The winds have strengthened and we are in for a stormy night.

Sleep proves almost impossible as the storm rages through the night. I am up before dawn when I hear the snowplough. It is before 6 a.m. but the maintenance crew are out ploughing our drive. How thankful we are to have this service! I vividly recall another winter when we spent four hours clearing a snow-covered driveway, where the snow was so deep that my car was completely buried.

Strong winds are forecast by Environment Canada, but I don't need to read the forecast to know what is happening all around us. There are gusts up to 100 km/h/60 mph. Last night's rain has washed away much of the snow and the temperature is still above freezing but is set to plummet for the weekend. Welcome to winter in Canada!

I read in the news that the Island is almost surrounded by ice, which is unusual for this time of year, according to the Canadian Coast Guard. The recent frigid temperatures have contributed to the early ice development, which is up to 30 centimetres/12 inches thick in the Northumberland Strait and around the Confederation Bridge. What is particularly unusual is the fact that there is thicker ice forming on the north side of Prince Edward Island, in the colder, deeper waters of the Gulf of Saint Lawrence. This is due to the overspill of ice from the Northumberland Strait.

When major winter storms arrive, they cause the ice to shift and break up due to storm surges, but it is quick to re-form because the heat has gone from the shallower waters of the Strait at this time of year.

Outside, clearing snow proves to be harder than anticipated. Although the rain washed away most of the snow from the garden, the areas of greatest accumulation were the drive and path. The drive was ploughed, but the residue of heavy, wet snow is compacting and starting to freeze due to the sheering force of the wind. Shovelling is hard work, as the heavy snow clings to the shovel and is so difficult to move. The wind is gusting so strongly that it is challenging managing to stay upright and Mr Candytuft falls twice on the slippery driveway but is, thankfully, unhurt. I clear the snow from the front path and struggle to stay on my feet due to the slippery path and the buffeting winds. I am relieved to finish the path and return indoors. I have no intention of venturing out again today in these dangerous conditions.

The brutal cold continues for another couple of days, with wind chills of minus 33°C. I listen to the BBC and hear them talking of 'bitter cold' with temperatures of minus 2°C in the UK. They really don't have a clue what bitter cold actually feels like.

I'm back at the track today and there is a sign outside, which reads, 'Help us to keep the track clean. Please wipe your feet on the mat provided, like at grandma's house.' Most walkers bring shoes to change into these days, but boots tramp in lots of salt from slippery outdoor surfaces.

We drive home through town, where there are mountains of snow piled high on either side of the street, where the parking areas have been ploughed. The road is slushy and very slippery, as the wind has blown the snow back onto it. We skid to a halt at a traffic light. We head out of town and return home. It isn't really the weather for any but essential stops: even in boots, the conditions are sloppy and dangerous underfoot. I've been wearing my Nordic Grips on my boots for a couple of days now, as I don't want to slip and fall in the icy conditions.

It snows overnight and we wake to about 20 centimetres/8 inches of fresh, powdery snow. The weather is mild enough that I want to get out for some fresh air. It takes me about twenty minutes to clear the snow off the car before I can even think about going out. I drive into town and head for my favourite walk along the harbour front. I am early today because I have arranged to chat with a friend in Norway this morning. With the time difference of five hours, we usually chat late morning (local time).

I've even beaten the snow plough this morning, so I arrive to find I'm wading about in snow. However, undeterred, I make for where the trail lies hidden beneath the snow and set off. The air is fresh and the wind minimal, which means it is a lot milder than of late.

Walking in the snow is quite challenging, so I opt to walk part of the way along the road. I return to the trail further down, where it disappears into the trees, which are laden with fresh snow. It looks so pretty today, but I don't have the camera with me. I'm sure there will be other photo opportunities before winter is over.

My legs get a good workout as I plod through the snow. There is only one other walker this morning and he is equipped with poles. I'm managing to stay upright, though the trail is slippery in places. Reaching the end of the trail, I hear an engine noise behind me and turn to make the return trip as the snowplough arrives. I wave at the driver and he waves back. Once he has passed me, I am able to continue. Whilst it is nice to have a clear path, it is a bit more slippery after the plough has been through. I suddenly realise I am being a bit over-confident and slow down: I am wearing Nordic Grips on my boots, but they don't provide a lot of traction in slushy conditions.

I get back to the car and head towards home. The road conditions are poor and the car skids slightly on a couple of occasions, but nothing too dramatic. After years of winter driving, I am accustomed to the challenges faced when venturing out on the roads. When I first moved to Canada, Mr Candytuft bought me a session at Skid School, which was a lot of fun, but also taught me how to drive in hazardous winter conditions.

The snow starts again in the afternoon: fine flakes at first, but becoming gradually heavier. The world is silent. I watch through the window as it continues to fall. I'm supposed to be working on writing this book, but I am staring at the view out of the window, which is like a giant snow globe. Someone has shaken my world and I'm watching as it rearranges itself.

An unexpected mild front passes through and the temperature

reaches 10 C. Weather like this is far too rare to miss, so I'm back at the boardwalk this morning. Mr Candytuft is out of commission again, due to his ongoing knee problem. I may be walking alone, but I'm enjoying being out in the fresh air.

It is very wet underfoot, due to the rapid thaw, and the boardwalk is swamped. The adjacent trail is slightly less so. There are a few other walkers this morning, but not as many as might otherwise have decided to head out, due to strong westerly winds, which make for challenging conditions. I certainly get my fill of fresh air and healthy exercise.

The following morning is even milder, as the mercury climbs to 13°C. It is the weekend and our neighbourhood is quiet. I head out for a walk before the arrival of forecasted bad weather later in the day. I walk for an hour and see only one other person on foot – a runner – it seems most of my neighbours would rather be indoors, even on such a mild morning. All of the snow has disappeared due to the rapid thaw, and the huge piles of snow, which were left by the ploughs, have vanished.

It is quite challenging to make any progress on this walk, as it is another windy day with strong southerly gusts. I battle along with my head down, striding purposefully, to make any progress. I arrive home not long before the weather closes in: the darkening sky spreads from the west and we watch the progress of this front from our living room window.

Environment Canada is busy issuing warnings of a flash freeze and, within a couple of hours, the rain starts and there is a rapid drop in temperature. The forecast is for 40 millimetres/1.5 inches of freezing rain. We are glad to be safe at home.

We don't venture out for two days: when we do go out, we find everything covered in a thick layer of ice. It is almost impossible to stand up outside without holding onto something for support. Mr Candytuft spends about thirty minutes trying to get the ice off the car windscreen (even with the aid of a heated screen).

I'm still braving the cold to get outdoors for morning exercise on the days when it isn't absolutely freezing. I find these walks far more beneficial for my physical and mental health than mindlessly doing circuits of the walking track. Even on days of sub-zero temperatures, I see people of all ages doing the same – from babes in arms to seniors with walking sticks – they are a hardy breed here on Prince Edward Island.

Back in the kitchen, I'm making Scotch broth with homemade lamb stock, which simmered in the slow cooker all day yesterday. I spend ages chopping carrots and swede into tiny cubes and adding chopped celery, onions and pearl barley to the stock. The soup then simmers in the slow cooker for a further eight hours. This may be slow food, but it is the perfect winter meal: warming, comforting and nourishing.

We wake to a thick layer of fresh snow blanketing the landscape and icing the dark firs of the garden. The snow started yesterday afternoon and continued into the night. In the early hours my sleep was disturbed by the noise of the snowploughs clearing roads and driveways. School start time has been delayed by an hour to allow everyone extra time to get in after the snow. Weather conditions have to be fairly severe before school is cancelled.

We go out to clear the paths and drive, and Mr Candytuft clears the car. Before this, I'm outside taking photos of the winter wonderland scene. Much as I dislike digging out, I still see the magic of a day like today. There are about 30 centimetres/12 inches of snow to clear and I'm glad of my waterproof clothing and boots, though my gloved hands soon get cold moving the snow with a shovel.

Once completed, we get ready and head into town. Traffic is moving normally and everyone is getting on with their day without any fuss.

We go to the supermarket for some groceries and I discover Storm Chips, which I've heard of, but never actually seen. These potato chips (crisps) were released about two years ago by the Covered Bridge Potato Chip Company of New Brunswick and they have become a Maritime phenomenon, being almost exclusively sold in the Atlantic provinces. Described as a 'flurry of flavours', they have been marketed mainly through social media. Each bag contains their four most popular flavours: Smokin' Sweet BBQ, Homestyle Ketchup, Creamy Dill and Sea Salt & Vinegar, 'To keep your taste buds warm with flavour no matter how cold it is outside.' This perfect blend of flavours is packaged in a winter-themed bag featuring potatoes dressed for winter in hats and scarves.

An article featured in *The Globe and Mail* on 24 January 2017 noted: 'Maritimers can tell when a storm is on the horizon by the state of the snack-food aisle. Chip shelves are ravaged, with a few forlorn bags left askew in the wake.' Along with the usual essentials, such as bottled water, bread and milk, the only way to see out a big winter storm is with a good supply of Storm Chips. Supermarkets are now prepared for each forecasted winter storm, buying extra supplies of Storm Chips and even clearing shelf-space to allow for additional stock.

I buy a bag, purely in the interest of research. Mr Candytuft says he doesn't want chips but soon changes his mind once I open them. They are good. I only hope there aren't too many winter storms in the weeks to come, as they won't be good for our waistlines!

I read a report in our local paper that the local Salvation Army Christmas Kettle Campaign raised over $43,000 during the weeks leading to Christmas and that, across the Maritimes, they raised $1.86 million. Over 300,000 Maritimers are low-income families and many thousands live in poverty. The success of the Salvation Army's fundraising activities is due to the commitment of the many volunteers who give their time to stand by a kettle and ring their bells, and to the generosity of the Maritime community. The donated money will be used to provide the basic necessities of life – food, clothing and shelter – to those in need.

It is Saturday morning and I'm debating whether to go for a walk at the track. I'm really not trying too hard to convince myself that I want to go out, because we are in another deep freeze and it is cosy and warm indoors. I watch the snow blowing off the trees in the garden and give an involuntary shiver. Why would I want to go out on such a cold day? I'm still feeling guilty about not getting enough exercise, when the weather takes a sudden turn for the worse: it starts snowing again and big flakes are quickly settling. Now I'm convinced that my best option is to stay at home.

Mr Candytuft suddenly decides he can't last the weekend without a supply of tonic water and heads outside to de-ice the car, which is a lengthy job these days, due to the accumulation of snow and ice.

Later, I'm upstairs when he calls me to come urgently. I'm wondering what the panic is until I get to the living room to be told there is a skunk in the garden. We watch as it makes its way between the trees at the bottom of the garden, which it is using for cover. I try to take some photos but it is too far away and the photos are disappointing.

I do some research and discover that this black and white mammal, which is about the size of a domestic cat, is a member of the weasel family. It has a stout body, a small head, short legs, a bushy tail and thick, glossy-black fur. The distinctive white stripe down the centre of its head forks at the shoulders; then continues as white stripes down each side of its back. This is the Eastern Striped Skunk.

Skunks are generally nocturnal creatures so I'm not sure what this one is doing out in the middle of the day. I also learn that they hibernate in winter, so this one really shouldn't be out and about in January.

For those of you who are unfamiliar with skunks, the reason for their bad reputation is their ability to spray from their anal scent glands: when faced with an imminent threat, a skunk will arch its back, raise its tail and start foot stomping, before spraying their distinctive musk to warn off any predator. Get in their way at your peril: if sprayed, it is extremely difficult to eradicate their scent.

Skunks were highly valued for their pelts and were introduced to Prince Edward Island by fur farmers around 1915. They multiplied and established themselves in the wild throughout the Island where, despite attempts to control their numbers through bounty payment schemes in the 1930s and 1940s, they survive to this day.

I was already aware we had skunks in the neighbourhood because I had smelled them in the garden – not that 'in your face' stink of freshly sprayed musk, which I can only describe as being a bit like burned rubber, only stronger – merely a faint odour that told me they were around.

Well, my approach is 'live and let live'. They aren't doing me any harm and they do look rather cute. I wish I had managed to capture a decent photo to share with family and friends.

***

I've been reading about what makes for a happy society and one of the most important factors is trust. Meik Wiking is the CEO of the Happiness Research Institute in Copenhagen and author of *The Little Book of Lykke*. He writes about the lost wallet experiment, where wallets containing a small amount of cash, photos and a couple of personal items were dropped in various city locations around the globe, including Toronto. This experiment challenged the theory that most people are honest and will take the trouble to return a lost wallet if they find it. In fact, eighty per cent of wallets dropped in Toronto were returned intact.

A similar experiment was set up in Atlantic Canada shortly before Christmas, by the region's credit unions. Twelve wallets were left in public places across the four Atlantic provinces. The credit unions believed that the values of honesty, trust and fairness are alive and well in the region and they wanted to test their theory.

Each wallet contained $100 cash, a debit card, receipts and a contact number. Within hours of the start of the experiment, the calls were coming in. Nine of the wallets were returned with all of their contents intact. The credit unions don't know what happened to the other wallets but think they may still be out there, waiting for someone to find them.

They were impressed with the honesty of the people who found and returned the nine wallets and were pleased to report that, 'East coast folks get a passing grade in the good Samaritan test.'

When asked, most of those who returned the wallets said they know the hassle of replacing identification cards and they wouldn't want it to happen to them. As a thank you for their honesty, the good Samaritans were allowed to keep the money, whilst the credit unions made a donation to charities of the finders' choice. Some of the good Samaritans chose to top-up the charitable donation with the money from the wallet, which the credit union representative said, 'Speaks to who we are as Atlantic Canadians.'

There are various degrees of trust, and living here has certainly opened my eyes. Growing up in a place where we wouldn't leave the door unlocked, even when at home, and where part of the routine of going out was checking that the windows were securely locked, I find that people here rarely lock their doors and are quite happy to go out and leave the windows open (though not in January!). How else would callers be able to drop anything off, if they were not at home?

It is not unusual to discover a parcel left on the kitchen table – this actually happened to Mr Candytuft when we previously lived in Nova Scotia, where mail was delivered to our house, when he came out of the shower to find that the postman had been. Where else but the Maritimes? Clearly, the postman had knocked and when no one answered, he tried the door, then walked in and made the delivery.

Mr Candytuft still gets upset with me because I lock the door if I'm alone in the house, but old habits die hard. We do still lock the doors when we leave the house.

Then there is the issue of cars – rarely locked around here. In cold weather, I've seen cars parked and left with their engines running whilst their owners go about their business – not good for the environment, but I suppose the owners return to warm cars. Most people leave their keys in the ignition and often leave the windows wide open in the summer. The interesting aspect of all this is that they get away with it – they trust that the majority of people are honest and won't take what is not theirs.

Even around the homes and gardens of the neighbourhood, there are plenty of items left outside – sometimes for weeks – and they are still there when their owners go looking for them. This happens with garden furniture, bikes and children's toys, to name but a few items.

When we go to the walking track, we leave our coats and boots like everyone else and go for a walk. They are still there waiting for us when we return. I actually managed to leave my boots behind one day recently and went home in my walking shoes. I only realised what I had done when I got home. Mr Candytuft kindly volunteered to go back for them (it was a freezing, cold day) and they were still where I had left them.

Living on Prince Edward Island, there is a real sense of community and togetherness. A small population means there are multi-layered relationships – people know one another, either because they are related, they went to school with one another, they are neighbours, they work together, or they are the friend of a friend. Everywhere, people look for connections and through these connections, there is that bond of trust.

Perhaps this explains why Canada ranked seventh in the 2017 World Happiness Report of the world's twenty happiest countries. Countries were ranked according to per capita GDP, social support, life expectancy, 'perceptions of corruption' and freedom to make life choices. By comparison, the UK came in at nineteenth, with long commutes to work, particularly in urban areas, and an unequal work/life balance given as the reasons.

But it seems Canadians are not as happy as they used to be: a ranking of seventh in 2017 is Canada's lowest ranking since the Happiness Index began in 2012. Canada normally ranks fifth or sixth.

Norway took the top spot: a caring society, freedom,

generosity, health, income and good governance all contribute to keeping Norwegians happy. The top ten countries all rank highly in aspects of income, healthy life expectancy, having someone to count on in times of trouble, generosity, freedom and trust.

On a local level, one of the most contentious issues affecting Islanders on a daily basis is the exorbitant toll fee to cross the Confederation Bridge to the mainland. The fees for crossing are reviewed and increased annually and the toll rose to $47.00 for a car crossing, at the beginning of January. Add in the cost of fuel and this makes any off-island travel unaffordable to many. This is the reason why, in the six months that we've been residents, we have only been to the mainland once.

In the local paper I read about an online petition to abolish the toll. This petition was created by a woman who had to receive medical treatment, involving a hospital stay, on the mainland. Her family and friends were considerably out of pocket with the expense of toll fees each time they wanted to visit her. The petition was started in June 2015, but lost momentum after two years, however, the recent toll increases have garnered new interest and the petition received over 2,000 new signatures during the course of a few days. To date, there are more than 23,000 people who want to see the toll removed or, at the very least, discounted for Islanders.

I head over to the online petition, where I read there is no fee to cross the new Champlain Bridge in Montreal, which cost $1 billion, so why are Islanders being so unfairly treated? The Confederation Bridge is run by a private company, which has a contract until 2032, at which point it will pass into the hands of the federal government. Even if they then decide to remove the toll charges, that still leaves Islanders paying for the next fourteen years.

Medical care has been much on my mind lately because Prince Edward Island has a chronic shortage of doctors. We found we were unable to register with a family doctor when we arrived here and that wasn't only due to the three-month waiting period for a new health card. When I asked about finding a doctor, I was directed to the Patient Registry, where those seeking one add their names to the list. We are in good company too, as there are around 8,000 Islanders without a family doctor and little hope of finding one any time soon. I talked to one woman who moved here from Ontario four years ago and she only managed to register with a doctor about six months ago: this doctor is not even in her local community but if she had declined she would have found herself back at the end of the waiting list.

Not having a family doctor makes accessing health care interesting. I recently went for some routine screening only to be questioned about my lack of a physician. When I explained that we had only recently moved to the province, I was told to add my name to the Registry. I've also tried approaching a doctor's office and asking to register and asking other health care professionals, only to be met with the stock answer of, 'We are not accepting new patients.'

Recruitment of doctors to the province is not even keeping up with natural wastage. Family physicians are an ageing population and as they retire, any new recruits have to take over their existing caseload, leaving no room for patients on the Registry waiting list.

In an attempt to alleviate some of the health issues of our local community, a medical clinic opened here before Christmas. It is staffed by a Registered Nurse, who initially offered health screening for diabetes and chronic lung problems. We visited her office and had a chat about the doctor shortage and I asked if there are any plans to recruit Nurse Practitioners (NPs), but NPs cannot currently work independently in this province: they can only see the patients who are registered with a physician in the practice where they are employed. This seems so lacking in vision, as NPs offer excellent care and could make up for the shortfall in physicians, meaning that many of the people on the waiting list could have access to the care they need, rather than relying on visits to walk-in clinics where the focus is on getting them through as quickly as possible.

As we head into the final week of January, there has been another upward swing in temperature. The thermometer reading is 5°C and it feels like spring after weeks of cold weather. There has been a sudden overnight thaw and the snow has almost completely disappeared.

I head down to the harbour, where the water has reappeared for the first time in more than a month, although much of the bay is still covered in ice. The saturated ground cannot absorb the water and large pools have formed, attracting seabirds and crows, which are having a bath! Everywhere there is the sound of running water heading towards the shore.

People are out enjoying the day. It doesn't take much of a temperature rise to get everyone outdoors. After weeks of sub-zero temperatures, 5°C feels like a heatwave.

An hour of fresh air and exercise leaves me feeling invigorated: the blue sky and sunshine is a real treat after prolonged periods of overcast, grey skies. As I head back to the car, a red squirrel runs up to me, looking for treats. I haven't seen the squirrels recently, so they must have been in hibernation.

I am not home for long before the weather takes a dramatic turn for the worse. Plunging temperatures cause another rapid freeze and it starts to snow again. Winter is not quite ready to loosen its grip.

It is late afternoon at the end of January when the ferocity of the latest winter storm unleashes. We have been on a storm watch for two days as a low-pressure system tracked north-east: the direction of the dreaded Nor'easters, which typically bring very heavy rain or, at this time of year, snow.

The wind started early and has been howling around the house. Mr Candytuft went out this morning to find our snow shovels, which had been left by the back door, in the middle of the drive. Heavy freezing rain follows, which lashes the back of the house, obliterating our view. Our windows are now opaque, like frosted glass. I've been prowling around, peering out through the gaps in an attempt to see what is happening. I feel like a caged tiger stalking the perimeter in a bid to escape: I've got cabin fever from too much time indoors. This is mainly due to the fact that I have strained my back and, after trying to continue as normal, I've had to stop exercising and rest, as my back is getting worse. Enforced rest has kept me indoors for the past week.

What snow there is so far is swirling and eddying around the house, blown by the wind. The storm is forecast to continue until tomorrow.

We wake to another windy dawn. There is some limited visibility at daybreak, but much blowing snow. The wind is picking it up and causing it to swirl across the fields, creating a white mist close to the ground. Above this, the sky is clearing and the storm has passed.

We stay at home and read stories in the media, which are full of the blue moon and the imminent eclipse. The expression 'Once in a blue moon' used to puzzle me when I was a child, but I now know that a blue moon occurs in a month when there are two full moons. Not only is there a blue moon this month, but it is a supermoon and the stories are about this 'super blue blood moon eclipse'. We are in the wrong part of the country to witness this lunar eclipse, as the moon is setting in our part of the world at the time when the eclipse is forecast to begin. Not only that, but we also have no visibility on the western horizon, so we also miss the supermoon.

The wind continues to blow throughout the day. We remain indoors and are thankful that the power is still working, as such winds often cause hydro poles to come down (most electricity cables are above-ground), leading to power cuts, or 'outages' as they refer to them here.

CHAPTER SIX

FEBRUARY: COMMUNITY

The winter weather continues as the calendar rolls around to February. The second day of February is Groundhog Day in Canada and the United States. A 'weather prediction' is given based on whether a groundhog, emerging from its den, sees its shadow. According to legend, if the groundhog sees its shadow, we can expect another six weeks of winter.

Nova Scotia's groundhog, Shubenacadie Sam, predicted a faster onset of spring than his 'cousin' Wiarton Willie, in Wiarton, Ontario, who saw his shadow. This agreed with Punxsutawney Phil of Pennsylvania when he saw his shadow.

If you think about it, it isn't much of a prediction, as we are actually at the mid-point between the winter solstice and the spring equinox, so we can expect another six weeks of winter. I would like to think that it will actually be over in six weeks, but I suspect it will be longer than this before spring arrives.

The temperatures continue to fluctuate and we have a very crisp, cold Saturday morning in early February. The sky is blue, tinged with pink and the temperature is minus 18°C, but the strong wind means a wind chill of minus 28°C. Another flash freeze has glazed surfaces and made them as slippery as the local ice pad. We stay indoors and hibernate throughout the weekend.

A sudden rise in temperature at the start of the week, together with overnight rain, has seen the snow melting, resulting in widespread flooding of roads and pavements. Ice-blocked culverts have pushed water onto the road and there is a stream running down the path opposite our house. Our garden is swamped and mostly underwater.

Mr Candytuft and I venture into town as I feel in need of exercise. I haven't walked on a regular basis for almost two weeks since I strained my back. I would love to walk outdoors on this mild morning, but it is still icy in places and I don't want to further aggravate my back by slipping on the ice.

We head to the track, where I end up cutting my walk short after my back starts bothering me again. A stop at the supermarket is called for, to buy a couple of items, and we spend far longer than necessary looking around. It is so good to be out of the house, as we have been indoors too much and are both in need of a change of scene. Options are somewhat limited at this time of year unless one wants to go shopping. The mild weather continues into the afternoon but, with the temperature forecasted to fall to minus 11°C by morning, it is going to be icy again.

A news story on CBC reports that Prince Edward Island has the second highest rate of hospital admissions, due to slips and falls on ice, in Canada. This comes as no surprise to me, as I've had my share of them. The maritime climate results in freezing rain causing icy conditions, sudden thaws and flash freezes, together with the sheering effect of strong Arctic winds, combining to make surfaces treacherous. Slipping on ice is considered a rite of passage in Canadian winters.

In an effort to brighten what is probably one of the most depressing times of the year when spring still seems so far away, I head into the kitchen to bake a treat. I decide to make an apple crumble with custard – real comfort food. I add oats to the topping (I'm trying to convince myself it is healthier than it is) and I use the apples we harvested in October, which I had stored as slices in the freezer. Once ready, I mix Bird's Custard powder with milk and make a fairly thick custard. This always reminds me of home and family, as it is one of the desserts that my mum used to make for us when we were young. We indulge in a little mid-week treat and both feel better. Mr Candytuft says it is the best apple crumble I've ever made. Roll on spring!

The next morning is cold, but I can't handle any more time indoors. I bundle up in thermals, fleece trousers, down jacket, hat, hood, scarf and gloves, and go for a walk at the harbour front. It is quite windy and cold, but the sun peeps out from behind the clouds and makes the effort worthwhile.

I cut my walk short because of the conditions underfoot. I manage to avoid the worst of the icy patches, but turn back when I reach a part of the trail that is sheltered from the sun and is still covered with ice.

***

A few days later, it is Mr Candytuft's birthday and we go for a walk along the harbour front. The day is crisp and there is a clear blue sky to the south. Dark clouds are forming to the north, which will bring yet another winter storm. The sky towards the horizon is cerulean blue fading to almost white and the colour reminds me of a watercolour painting. For once, it isn't windy, which means that, even though it is a cold day, the temperature feels more bearable.

We walk for a little over an hour and see a few red squirrels foraging for food. We offer one a peanut, but he is too timid to take it. An advance from his left flank finds another squirrel eyeing the reward. Now that competition has arrived, a chase ensues as each tries to see the other off. Meanwhile, a third squirrel arrives and claims the prize. He sits on his haunches and nibbles the peanut whilst the others try to move in and grab it, but he chatters at them and keeps them at a safe distance.

We see chickadees, which are similar in size to a blue tit, darting amongst the undergrowth and visiting the feeders. Someone has been along this morning and filled them with black nyjer seeds, which they are enjoying.

Once home again, I get busy in the kitchen, baking Mr Candytuft's birthday cake. I'm baking a fresh ginger cake from a recipe I've never tried before. I don't normally use fresh ginger, but this recipe comes highly recommended, so I think it is worth the effort of peeling, chopping and mincing the ginger.

The cake preparation itself seems to require a lot of utensils and the kitchen is a mess by the time it is ready for the oven. Once cooled, I plan to ice the cake with lemon icing and grated zest before adding a few birthday candles.

In the meantime, we prepare dinner – a beef stew – perfect for a cold winter evening. After we have eaten dinner, I light the candles and sing 'Happy Birthday'. Mr Candytuft blows them out and cuts into the cake and I remind him to make a birthday wish. I then cut generous pieces of cake, which we enjoy with a cup tea – Yorkshire Gold, of course. The cake is a hit, although Mr Candytuft observes that it would have been better with ice cream.

The snow starts during the evening – fine flakes coming down almost horizontally and obliterating the landscape. I look outside and I do not even see tyre tracks on the road. It looks like everyone is hibernating on this dark, snowy night.

The morning dawns with an overcast sky. The snow has ended, but it appears we had freezing rain at some point, which made the snow heavy and ice-crusted. We go outside and crunch through the top layer: it is very slippery underfoot. It takes ages to clear the car windows and the doors are frozen shut. We see our neighbour and all agree that we have had enough of winter. As she observes, 'Maybe it is time to move elsewhere.' My preference would be somewhere less cold and far less snowy.

It is a couple of days later and the morning is crisp and cold. The cloudless blue sky and sunshine belie quite how cold it is outdoors. The sun is shining on the snow-covered garden and it looks like millions of sparkling diamonds.

A trip into town begins with de-icing the car, which is always a lengthy process these days. The first challenge is actually managing to get the doors open as, once again, they are frozen shut. Mr Candytuft spends ages chipping away at the ice until we are able to go out. It is so cold that melted snow is refreezing in rivulets on the windscreen.

We go to the walking track and then stop to buy groceries on our way home. We are both freezing, despite layers of clothing. The wind chill is minus 17°C this morning, according to the forecast, but it feels much colder. It is with a sense of relief that we return home and spend the rest of the day indoors. This seems like such a long winter.

It is said that winter in Canada is not a season, but rather a test of endurance, and it's one I am clearly failing. Storm after storm is giving me as much of a battering as the environment. I now realise I'm not built for winter in Canada. I may have several years of Canadian winters behind me, but they never get any easier.

A Sunday morning in mid-February finds me trying to clear the car of snow and dig it out after yet another winter storm. There is a significant accumulation of snow because neither of us has felt able to clear up after the previous storm. This has added to the difficulty of trying to shift not only the fresh snow, but also the compacted ice layer beneath. I am only too aware of the fact that I've spent three weeks recovering from a back strain and I don't want to aggravate it further, so I'm taking it steady; pausing to rest and making sure I bend my knees and keep my back straight. As far as possible, I'm trying to push the snow out of the way, but at certain points, it is necessary to lift the shovel and when I do so, I find out exactly how much effort is required to move this heavy, wet ice, which sticks to the shovel, even when I try to remove it.

The wind picks up and stings my face: I have to get a scarf for protection. The moisture from my breathing is making my scarf damp, but it can't be helped. My hands are cold too, as my gloves are getting wet from shovelling. One thing is going through my mind: I can't take another Canadian winter.

I tackle the front steps, where I am knee-deep in snow. I have to feel for the steps with my shovel, as I can't see them. The front path is the worst part of the job, with the heaviest snow but, finally, the job is done and I can retreat indoors to thaw out. Despite waterproof over-trousers and boots, in addition to all of my other protective winter clothing, I'm cold and my legs are freezing. It takes two cups of tea before I start to feel human again.

The next morning is mild and I am determined to get outdoors for a walk. I head to town and go for a walk along the harbour, but this proves to be more challenging than at first glance, as the trail is icy. I end up walking on the road, as all of the access paths to the trail are covered in sheet ice. The conditions make walking difficult and I have to dig my heels in with each step, in order to get some grip from my Nordic Grips and avoid slipping. It takes me fifty minutes to cover about two-thirds of the distance of my usual walk. Once I am back at the car I realise how much tension I have in my neck and back from trying to maintain my balance.

I think of a recent conversation I had with my mum in the UK. She told me there are already signs that spring is on its way. What am I doing here?

***

Shrove Tuesday falls on the 13 of February this year. It is named for its religious significance and is a day of feasting before the fasting of Lent. It is more commonly known these days as Pancake Day. Eating pancakes is another tradition that takes me back to childhood when my mother made them for us. I like to continue this tradition and so I spend time in the kitchen mixing pancake batter, which I leave to rest in the fridge until lunchtime. Mr Candytuft prefers his plain, but I indulge in a sweet treat and spread Nutella on mine. The warmth of the pancakes causes the chocolate spread to melt and they are delicious.

The following evening, I am standing in the kitchen preparing dinner when I glance out of the window and see the sky to the west turning pink. It is Valentine's Day and I want to capture the moment. I go to the front door and stand in the open doorway to take a photograph. The evening air is crisp and cold and we are expecting a severe frost tonight.

Back in the kitchen, I watch as the sky undergoes a dramatic change to near purple, fading to pink and orange towards the horizon. The high cirrus clouds are wispy and ripple across the sky: they have the mousse-like, light and airy quality of Angel Delight. I return to the doorway to take another photo and encourage Mr Candytuft to come and look at this beautiful sunset but he is half-comatose in the chair and won't get up. It seems that romance is dead: no watching the sunset together in our house. Finally, the sun disappears beyond the horizon and leaves the last remnants of pink tinges in the sky, as darkness falls.

***

The sense of community here is one of many factors that make Prince Edward Island a special place to live. Yesterday, there was a house fire in our neighbourhood, which left a family of seven in need. An appeal for help went out and so this morning, I am sorting clothing and personal care items to donate. We drop them off at the designated collection point, where we run into the housing manager. She tells us she was able to re-house the family in temporary, furnished accommodation and she will have a permanent home for them within a month. Not only this, but the maintenance crew will salvage their furniture from the smoke-damaged upper floor of the house and put it in dry storage to air out, then clean everything ready for their new home. Everyone is rallying round to do what they can to help this family in need.

I later read in the local paper that the mother and three youngest children were at home at lunchtime when a pan of oil caught fire. Thankfully, they all got out safely, together with their dog. Sadly, their cat didn't survive. The two older children were at school and their father was at work. The prompt actions of a passing police officer assisted the woman in getting her children to safety and, by the time the fire brigade arrived, the main floor was engulfed in smoke and flames.

A crowdfunding page is launched by family and friends of the displaced family and the donations will go to help them with their expenses. The most important factor in this tragic situation is that the family are all safe.

As the day is fine and mild, we go out for a change of scene and a drive to the town of O'Leary. I have an ulterior motive for wanting to go, as I know there is a craft shop in the town. Mr Candytuft is happy to go along with the plan, as there aren't many places to visit in winter.

This is the first time I've been to this part of the Island and, as we head westwards, we pass farms and snow-covered fields. There are swampy areas close to the roadside, distinguishable by the stunted trees. Everything is dull grey, as the trees sleep through the winter, although there are some firs dotted about, giving a hint of dark green to the landscape. The sun is shining, which makes everything better.

When we arrive in O'Leary, it isn't difficult to find the shop, which is located on the main street. We step out of the car without coats and walk a short distance to the entrance. It may only be 2°C but it feels like spring, after the cold we have experienced in recent weeks.

The shop is quiet and we chat to the woman about relocating to Prince Edward Island and places where we have lived. She mentions yesterday's fire, as she read about it in the local paper. We talk about community support and she tells us about a benefit (fundraising event) in a neighbouring community, which raised $6,000 to aid another local family. The funds will be used to assist with medical, travel and living expenses associated with the cost of specialist treatment in Toronto, for a baby girl with cancer. We chat about how rural communities rally together to help those in need.

We go to Tim Hortons for a light lunch before heading back

towards home. This fast food restaurant is a Canadian institution, best known for its coffee and 'donuts'. As I am neither a coffee drinker nor a fan of doughnuts, one might well ask what I am doing here. I settle for a cup of herbal tea and yoghurt, whilst Mr Candytuft has a soup and sandwich followed by two oatcakes (loaded with sugar!) and a coffee.

It is Roll up the Rim to Win season, which is an annual Tim Hortons'event, in which cups mean prizes (sometimes). Most of the time, I see the message 'please play again' hidden under the rim of the disposable cup. I've had inside information that the big prizes (cars, televisions etc) are on the large and extra-large size cups, so it is little wonder that I've never won anything more than a free drink, as I don't order half or three-quarter litre drinks.

Our plan is to return home via the scenic route along the shore, but Mr Candytuft doesn't believe in a GPS and seldom refers to a map. We reach the shore at West Cape and turn south. We try to reach the lighthouse at West Point, but the road isn't ploughed beyond the last house and we have to turn back. We pass the Harbourside Centre, which is closed, and see the frozen West Point harbour, with boats hauled out for winter. Soon after, we follow the road inland and we don't see the shore again. There are no easily accessible routes along the shore, a fact Mr Candytuft would have known, had he referred to a map. Still, it is nice to be out and about, though we have had the best of the weather. The sky is becoming overcast and the sun is barely visible by the time we reach home.

It is Flag Day. I discovered this from a reference to the fact on my calendar. I can't claim to have known that we even had a flag day and it seems to have escaped Mr Candytuft's notice, too. The 15 February is the 53rd birthday of the Maple Leaf. On 15 February 1965, the Maple Leaf was made the official flag of Canada, when it was raised on Parliament Hill in Ottawa.

I suppose the fact that this anniversary falls in winter is the reason why it passes by without much fanfare; at a time when most Canadians are tucked up at home and not out celebrating.

They tend to celebrate on national holidays like Victoria Day and Canada Day when the Maple Leaf is much in evidence.

Islander Day falls on the third Monday in February: a fact that had vaguely registered at the beginning of the year, when I was adding dates to a calendar, but was instantly forgotten. It is only when we venture into town in the afternoon that we discover everyone has taken the day off for this provincial holiday.

In other parts of Canada, this day is known as Family Day, although it is not a recognised statutory holiday; meaning that the federal government does not observe this day. It is one of those odd holidays which originated in Alberta in 1990 but took a while to become established elsewhere. Ontario first observed it in 2008 and Prince Edward Island in 2009 but chose to call it Islander Day. The idea behind this holiday is for families to be able to spend time together and enjoy a mini winter break.

We decide to go for a walk whilst we are in town and discover that many people have had the same idea. People of all ages are out on this beautifully sunny afternoon. We turn our steps towards the lighthouse and enjoy being out in the fresh air. The wind is quite cold, but we are prepared to tolerate some mild discomfort to be outdoors. Everyone feels this need to be out after weeks of cabin fever from being trapped indoors by winter. People smile and greet one another, often with comments about the positive improvement in the weather.

***

A long overdue haircut finds us on the road to Charlottetown. The morning is cold and the sky clear blue. The winter sun is low in the sky, necessitating frequent repositioning of the sun visor. I find the glare strong, even with sunglasses.

The snow has almost completely gone after a sudden thaw earlier in the week but, in its place, the field margins and verges have turned to sheet ice where the melt-water has refrozen. The fields themselves look a dull grey-brown except for areas where the Prince Edward Island red earth is visible. The dark firs look almost black on this winter morning.

After my appointment and a couple of errands, we make the return trip, passing the aptly named Eureka Garlic farm en route. I have to smile when I see this sign as, clearly, the owner has a sense of humour.

Heading back towards Summerside, we pass through the community of Travellers Rest. This always reminds me of a Yorkshire pub of the same name, which I visited on occasion. It always conjures an image of a cosy bar and subdued conversation in the days before big screen televisions became substitutes for engaging in conversation on an evening out.

We both miss real English pubs. If we venture into a pub or bar here, they lack the atmosphere of a traditional pub and most feel like restaurants that are trying too hard to be something else.

***

It is five months since we have been to the mainland, so there is a sense of relief to be heading in the direction of the Confederation Bridge on this fine morning in late February. The weather is perfect: brilliant blue sky, sunshine and good visibility make this an ideal day for such a trip.

We see distant clouds hugging the shore as we drive up onto the bridge. This is our first winter crossing of the Northumberland Strait, so we are interested to see how different it looks, in comparison to our previous crossings in summer.

There is a lot of ice in the Strait, but it is not completely frozen: areas of open water attract seabirds and the ice shifts with the tides. Mr Candytuft jokes that we are leaving 'terra flota' and returning to terra firma. I hadn't thought of it like this, but it is an apt description. Although not technically floating, we have been surrounded by water for seven months.

We stop at the same service area we last visited in September. It is quiet today as there are no tourists at this time of year. Mr Candytuft wants his 'hungry man's breakfast', whilst I choose a bowl of warming soup with warm bread.

Feeling refreshed, we head to Moncton to do our bulk shop. We are on a healthy eating campaign (or we will be, once we start it at the beginning of March), so we end up with a very different basket of groceries to our normal shopping. We buy lots of fish and lean chicken but are eliminating red meat. This is because Mr Candytuft is concerned about winter weight gain due to the inclement weather, and too much time spent in his La-Z-Boy recliner.

We visit a couple of other places before our return trip. We are back on the highway and heading towards home by 4.30, by which time the weather has changed and is more overcast.

The clouds are stunning as we head back across the bridge. The sun is starting to set in the west (behind us) and I'm straining to take photos of the beautiful sky, but hampered by my seatbelt. The sun is shining behind the clouds, which are indigo blue fading to white. All of the colours are being reflected off the ice surface and the water.

We turn west as we head back onto the Island. The photo opportunities continue and I'm busy taking shots of the horizon with the trees and buildings in sharp relief against the pinks, mauves, lilacs and oranges of the setting sun. We reach home as the sun sets. It has been an absolutely stunning sunset and I feel so lucky to have experienced it first-hand.

CHAPTER SEVEN

MARCH: CABIN FEVER

The weather seems to be gradually improving as we head into March (although I hate to tempt fate by stating this aloud). The nights are still cold with sub-zero temperatures, but we have had a couple of days where the temperature has crept above freezing.

One such morning sees us heading to the boardwalk for some much-needed exercise. The past couple of weeks have seen us vegging out at home watching box sets on the television, with no motivation to get outdoors in the cold, or even to go to the track. I've reached the stage where I can't bear the thought of plodding mindlessly round in circles and prefer to be out in the elements, if possible (provided it isn't too cold/wet/snowy).

The morning is perfect if a little windy. The sun is shining in a near-cloudless sky and the light is reflected off the still-frozen harbour. Thankfully, we both brought our sunglasses, as there is far too much glare without them.

Other walkers are out enjoying the morning and greetings are exchanged. We pause at the bridge over the little stream where we watched the muskrats last year. The stream is flowing and there are three mallard ducks squabbling and chasing one another. Could it be coming into the mating season?

A red squirrel runs up to Mr Candytuft, who gives it a nut.

Another approaches me and I stand perfectly still with a peanut in my hand. To my delight, the squirrel comes right up to me and takes the peanut from my fingers. I can't believe that I've just fed a red squirrel by hand!

The return trip is colder because we have the wind in our faces all the way back. It is with a sense of relief that we bundle ourselves into the car and head for home. It may be March and sunny, but the wind still has quite a bite to it.

The following week, we are back at the boardwalk on yet another cold, windy day. We pause on the bridge on the sheltered stretch where the muskrats live and we spot four of them in the stream. They are swimming and diving, then resurfacing and they put on quite a show. Other walkers pause to see what is happening and soon there are five of us (and a Labrador) watching them. This is the first time that we have seen them in months. The tide is out: the stream seems lower than normal and we spot the muskrats' den when one of them disappears into it. It is tucked into the bank of the stream and is normally hidden. Watching the muskrats is the highlight of our walk, though we do see lots of red squirrels about on our return to the car.

Environment Canada has been forecasting what they euphemistically describe as two 'weather events' for the end of the week. What they really mean is snow. It may be March, but winter is not finished with us quite yet.

We head out for a walk before the snow arrives. It is another cold day due to strong winds from the east. I'm better prepared for the cold today, with an extra thermal layer, after freezing during exercise on the previous two mornings.

We are heading along at a fair pace when a woman hails us and engages us in conversation. She is a visitor (who visits Prince Edward Island in winter?). She has a Boxer dog with her and we learn that she is dog-sitting for a few weeks. She has come all the way from Tennessee and admits to having visited before, but only in the summer. She is certainly seeing a very different side to it today.

I start to get cold and we move on. By the time we retrace our steps, she has disappeared. No doubt she went back to the place where she is staying to thaw out!

The snow is forecast to begin at lunchtime and it arrives right on cue. Tiny flakes to start, then getting gradually larger and accumulating on our (almost snow-free) garden and driveway.

I'm trying to stay positive and convince myself that spring is not far away. To this end, I've been browsing seed catalogues and thinking about starting a garden. At least I can think about starting some seeds indoors in the next couple of weeks. (Note to self to find out the last frost date before sowing.)

I'm sitting at my desk looking out at the winter landscape. The clouds have closed in and the snow is still falling. I really was fooling myself if I thought winter was going to let us off so easily.

The snow is less than predicted and the weather mild enough to go for a walk the following morning. There is very little wind, so being outside is a much more pleasant experience.

Down at the harbour, we find the ice has started to break up and there are now large patches of open water: the first we have seen in many months.

We head into town after our exercise, intending to stock up on a few groceries before the next storm. The shops are busy as everyone else seems to have had the same idea. There is something of a nesting instinct at work here – people want to be safe at home with all the necessities and no reason to venture outdoors.

The schools close two hours early, even though the snow has yet to start. According to the local news, the decision was taken this morning in order to avoid a repeat of the 'treacherous' road conditions yesterday.

The snow finally starts in the late afternoon and comes down thick and fast: gigantic flakes, which are quite different from those of yesterday's storm. They accumulate rapidly across the garden and driveway. It looks like another stormy night, as the wind starts blowing around the house.

Saturday morning sees a significant accumulation (10–15 cm/4-6 inches) of wet snow. I go out and start cleaning up, pacing myself as I shovel the snow off the deck and path. The snowplough arrives after I manage to get the car off the drive and I'm grateful for the assistance in moving the worst of it.

The weather is mild and a rapid thaw sets in as melt-water pours off the downspout onto the garden. The snow persists throughout the day but it is mainly intermittent flurries. We go for a short walk at dusk: although not warm outdoors, it feels good to get some fresh air.

The clocks go forward tonight, as we change to Daylight Savings Time (DST), otherwise known as Atlantic Summer Time, meaning that the evenings will be lighter next week. Although this change has occurred on the second Sunday of March since the US Energy Policy Act extended DST from 2007, I still feel that it is too early to make this change, as it occurs just as we have been enjoying the lighter mornings. From tomorrow, we will be waking to dark mornings again. The reason given for Canada making this change in line with the US is financial, as it is felt that it benefits cross-border trade when businesses are in the same time zone.

The Nor'easters continue, with two further storms bringing the total to three in six days. These are followed by unseasonably cold temperatures as we head into the third weekend of March. In between storms, we have cold, clear nights when the sky is full of stars. The Canadian Space Agency recommends Prince Edward Island National Park as being an amazing place for stargazing, but we don't need to travel to Cavendish to see bright stars – we can step outside our own door and look up. With low light pollution, the night-time sky is filled with stars, which sparkle like diamonds on the inky blackness of dark velvet: it is absolutely stunning.

Excitement has been mounting for the past few weeks as the jackpot for a local lottery, called Chase The Ice, has grown.

Chase The Ace is a fundraising idea which originated in Inuvik, Northwest Territories, which found its way to Nova

Scotia in 2013. Its success led to lotteries starting on Prince Edward Island in 2015. Tickets are sold and the jackpot accumulates each week. Fifty per cent of the money from ticket sales is kept for the charity, the weekly winning ticket holder gets twenty per cent and thirty per cent goes into the jackpot.

The lottery winner draws a card from a deck of playing cards, which are arranged face down on the table. The aim is to draw the ace of spades. If this is not drawn, the card selected is removed from the pack (and destroyed) and the game continues with the reduced pack of cards.

We were in Nova Scotia in 2015 and were present at the game in Inverness when the jackpot of $1.7 million was finally won. This game had run for over a year. The event drew crowds from all over the Maritimes and the community was swamped by large crowds as excitement reached fever-pitch.

Chase The Ice formed in 2017 when two not-for-profit groups with connections to (ice) hockey joined forces. The reason the lottery proved so popular is because it is the first one that was set up to allow online ticket sales.

The lottery jackpot reached $32,000 by the beginning of March and continued to grow week by week, as ticket sales increased and the number of remaining cards decreased. Ticket sales are boosted by sales at the Western Capitals' home games (the local hockey team). This week, the jackpot is estimated at $50,000 with only three tickets remaining. Like many other people, we are hoping for the call telling us our number is the winner, but we are disappointed.

You don't have to be physically present at the game, as they give you a call and allow you thirty minutes to reach the venue, or you may let someone else pick a card for you. Last week, the winning number was held by a Prince Edward Island resident who was working in Alberta. They called him and he told them which card he wanted them to turn over. He missed out on the jackpot, but still received the winning ticket prize of $4,890 (missing out on the $40,825 jackpot).

I look online and see that the game is over. The jackpot is

won by a syndicate of eight co-workers, who collect the $7,510 prize for the winning number, together with the $52,090 jackpot for finding the Ace of Spades. They split a total prize of $59,600 between them.

***

The equinox arrives, but there are still no signs of spring. I start sowing seeds indoors and try to be optimistic about spring's arrival and being able to start a garden. I spend hours studying seed catalogues and dreaming of an English cottage garden, with hollyhocks at the door. This part may turn into a reality if the plants I started from seed last summer have survived the winter outdoors.

Just when I'm thinking spring can't be that far away, the fourth Nor'easter in a little over three weeks arrives. The first signs of the impending storm are the strong, gusting winds. As the forecast has been warning of this storm for days, schools have remained closed: everyone is battening down the hatches in preparation for the arrival of the bad weather.

The snow starts around lunchtime and quickly obscures the view beyond our back garden as squall after squall blows in. The wind howls down either side of the house and the snow accumulates at the end of our drive and right across the road. We listen to the wind and are thankful to be indoors. Snow mixed with ice pellets rattles at the windows like handfuls of gravel being thrown at them: the storm rages around us. Periods of freezing rain follow, obscuring our view as the windows freeze over.

The weather forecast informs us that the winds are 80 km/h/50 mph which is Force 9, or a strong gale. Further north, on the western shore of Cape Breton, the winds are 128 km/h/80 mph which is Force 12 or hurricane-force.

The scene as night falls is of a winter landscape: snow-covered fields with heavy, blowing snow swirling across them. The storm rages on into the night.

I sleep surprisingly well considering the noise of the wind. Maybe it is because I am safe at home and can snuggle down under the duvet. I wake early to a still-dark sky. The wind speed has dropped, though it is still blowing. It is difficult to see what is happening outside when peering out into the darkness. I hear the plough go rumbling past and glance out of the window. At least the street will be clear for a while.

When dawn arrives, but there is no sign of the sun, as the sky is blanketed in a dull cloud. There is significant drifting where the wind has blown the snow across open ground. Our garden is a winter wonderland of deep snow, which reaches halfway up the post for our washing line. I look out of the window and see more movement as the snowploughs travel up and down, clearing the roads.

We are fortunate to have such a great service when it comes to snow ploughing. The crew get lots of practice and are very efficient at getting the streets and pavements cleared soon after the end of a storm. We have also been fortunate to have missed the heaviest of the winter snowfall of recent weeks.

There have been news reports on television of the snow in Bathurst, New Brunswick, which is only 300 km/186 miles from here, where there have been jaw-dropping amounts. The last storm dumped 40 cm/16 inches of snow on them, resulting in drifts as high as two-storey houses: some houses were completely buried. Residents were still digging themselves out four days after the latest storm. There was so much snow that tunnels were dug through the huge banks of drifts to allow pedestrians to walk in safety. Neighbours have helped one another with snow clearing, forming crews of people to help with digging out huge drifts, some of which were more than 5 metres/16 feet high. Life quickly returned to normal, though it will be many weeks before the snow disappears.

Friday is our day for 'residential waste collection', otherwise known to us as bin day (at least in our house). I only remember this after the snowplough has cleared our street. The rules state that our green cart for compostable waste must be at the curb by

7 a.m. I look at the Island Waste Management website to see if they are collecting today and see that normal service is continuing. I tell Mr Candytuft, whose job it is to take the bins out. He gets dressed in suitable clothing and boots and is in the process of doing so as the truck goes down the street. He barely gets the carts (our neighbour is away, so he takes her cart out as well) to the end of the drive, when the truck arrives.

Prince Edward Island is recognised as the leader in Canada for waste diversion and recycling. Islanders recycle almost double the Canadian average and we are proud of our attempts to keep recyclable or compostable material out of the landfill.

We go into town around lunchtime and find that all of the ice has disappeared from the harbour after last night's storm. It is the first time the harbour has been ice-free since early December. The harbour was completely frozen by Christmas Eve.

The snow has stopped, but the cold wind is blowing it across the road and we pass the snowploughs going into and out of town. It is a full-time job preventing further accumulation on the highway, which is the main route across the Island.

***

It is tax season: time for every Canadian to complete and submit their tax return for the previous year. I am the designated 'expert' when it comes to our household tax returns, as Mr Candytuft has absolutely no idea of how to complete a return and shows no inclination to learn. Most of my knowledge comes from trial and error and lots of time spent on the phone talking to Revenue Canada; with varying degrees of success. I've spent a lot of time this week waiting in call queues, listening to that awful music and generally becoming increasingly frustrated by misinformation.

The issue stems from a pension transfer and, as I am completing my return online, I almost have a heart attack when the tax software indicates a massive tax bill. So far, I've spoken to Revenue Canada four times: twice to senior agents. I've been in contact with the pension fund (twice); visited my bank three times and talked to two bankers; one of whom is a financial adviser. The only person who seems to have a grasp of the situation is the lovely lady at the pension fund, who has gone out of her way to assist me. This has taken up my entire week and it is yet to be resolved. As it is now 3 p.m. on Friday, I think it may be next week before I can continue and complete our returns.

Just when I think I will not hear anything further this week, the phone rings. It is the lady from the pension fund, calling to update me on progress. She has spoken to the bank directly on my behalf and they have found a solution. It seems the original pension transfer into the bank was processed incorrectly. In order to issue a tax receipt, the bank must first reverse the processing of the funds received before they can correct their error. I was beginning to think this would never be resolved in time, but must still wait for the new tax document.

***

I am up before dawn and it is still completely dark outside. The reason for getting up so early is because I'm starting work at 5.45 a.m. I had an interview last week and got a job at a local convenience store, which is in a neighbouring village. Part of my decision to look for a job is financial, as I have not had an income for two years, but I also feel that I need to get out of the house and do something productive with my time. After months of cabin fever, I believe that I need to get out and meet people if I am ever to feel part of the community. As jobs are few and far between here, the only option at this time is a job in retail.

The day passes in a blur as I struggle to learn about processing lottery tickets and identifying cigarette brands, all of which are in plain packaging and hidden away in drawers, as required by law. The store is busy and the work fast-paced. There is no opportunity to take a break and by the end of my shift, my head is spinning.

It is a beautiful afternoon, with sunshine and a sky of brilliant blue. The temperature remains below freezing and I wonder if this could be the calm before the storm, as I read about maritime folklore in today's paper. Apparently, Grandma says that there are three more snowfalls after the spring equinox. The first spring snow is the smelt snow when the smelts start to run. The second snow is the robin snow: folklore says that this snow heralds their return. The third and final snow is the green grass snow, otherwise known as the poor man's fertiliser.

Meteorologically speaking, March sees the jet stream attempting to move from its winter position to its summer position, as the seasons change. This may explain some of the other phenomena associated with Grandma's law and – just for the record – a lady told me she saw a robin in her garden today!

I'm up early again the following morning and it is a cold start to the day. Mr Candytuft de-ices the car and leaves the engine running as I get ready to leave for work. By the time we are ready to leave (less than ten minutes after he had scraped the windows), the windscreen has started to ice over again. The air is saturated with moisture and a heavy fog hangs over us. Visibility is significantly reduced as we head along the foggy highway.

When the sun rises, the scene that greets us looks like a visit from Jack Frost – a real winter wonderland of frosted trees – though rather unexpected in late March. The day is bright and sunny but continues cold. There is a general feeling that spring is imminent, if not actually here yet.

***

Ever since we arrived on Prince Edward Island, Mr Candytuft has wanted to eat more fish. We scoured the supermarkets for affordable options, but much of the fish sold is either previously frozen or produced in China. We are both adamant we want wild-caught, rather than farmed, fish and preferably from sustainable sources.

We bought wild-caught frozen fish on our trips to Moncton, but it isn't very convenient when our stock runs low, so Mr

Candytuft talks to the fishmonger in our local supermarket, who directs him to a place by the dock, which we had mistakenly believed, only sold shellfish. We pay them a visit and discover they sell locally caught fish from Nova Scotia: we buy about four kilos of fresh haddock and cod. They get fresh fish on a regular basis, so we don't have to rely on a freezer full of fish, though our purchases will go in the freezer for now.

The first hint of spring occurs two days before the end of March when the daytime temperature reaches 5°C and the sky is bright blue and sunny. Everyone has a spring in their step and a smile on their face. It feels like the season is changing and we have survived the worst that winter can throw at us.

Easter falls on the first Sunday after the first full moon after the spring equinox, which means that this year, it falls on 1 April. Although this is quite early, it can be as early as 22 March.

Good Friday finds me in the kitchen mixing dough for hot cross buns. The whole process of baking these is lengthy and cannot be rushed. The first rise takes an hour, so I cover the bowl and go and have a cup of tea. When the timer rings, I knock back the dough and then allow it to rise again for a further hour. At this stage, I take the dough from the bowl and divide it into a dozen buns, which I place on a baking tray. A third rise takes forty minutes, at which stage, I pipe crosses on them before placing them in the oven to bake. Once cooked, I glaze them whilst they are still warm and place them on a cooling rack, before putting the kettle on for afternoon tea with a cup of Yorkshire Gold – enjoyed with a still-warm and spicy bun, spread with melting butter – perfection!

We had planned to go out for fish and chips at lunchtime on Good Friday and had been looking forward to it for more than a week but, after a busy week, we completely forgot. Mr Candytuft remembers in the late afternoon, at around the time we are enjoying tea and buns. It is now too late to go, but there is no danger of us going hungry, with all that fish in the freezer!

The last day of March sees the return of the Canada geese

from their winter migration. The first warning of their arrival is their distinctive honking during flight, which I hear as they approach. I look out of the window and see three groups of them flying in formation, like Second World War Spitfires on a mission. As the geese have returned, maybe spring is about to start.

CHAPTER EIGHT

APRIL: ON THE ROAD AGAIN

Easter Sunday starts off cool and dull. The sun puts in an appearance for a while, but disappears behind a veil of thick cloud, as rain rolls in from the shore. I'm sitting at my desk writing and listening to the rain pattering on the roof: gently at first, but much heavier as it continues. It is breezy and we still have snow on the ground, but at least the rain should help to clear some of it.

I call my mum to wish her a happy Easter. She tells me that the weather in Yorkshire is very similar: cool, cloudy and breezy, with showers. Northern England is expecting snow tomorrow, so their winter isn't over yet, though they have had some milder spring days. The difference in the UK is that the daytime temperatures will be higher later in the week, so their snow won't last.

We celebrate Easter with a traditional British meal of roast leg of lamb. As we have been on our healthy eating plan for four weeks now, we haven't been eating red meat. We both enjoy our Easter treat and eat more meat than we have in weeks.

For some reason, lamb is not a popular choice for most Canadians, who seem to prefer turkey for any and every holiday meal. Although lamb is available in some supermarkets, it is mostly imported and bought by families whose cultural roots are outside Canada – mostly Europeans – especially Greeks.

Whenever I have mentioned that we eat lamb for our Easter meal, it seems to come as a surprise to many Canadians.

Locally produced lamb is available in season, but spring has yet to arrive here and we haven't seen any. The supermarkets have heavily promoted discounts on turkeys, though we do find an offer on legs of New Zealand lamb a few days before Easter and restock our freezer.

The first week of April sees very changeable weather with brief mild interludes before a return to minus 17°C daytime wind chills. The end of the week brings snowy conditions: winter is unwilling to release its icy grip.

News breaks of a horrific crash in Saskatchewan, after a bus carrying the Humboldt Broncos, a junior hockey team, collided with a truck on a rural highway. The stories that emerge over the following hours and days leave the whole of Canada in shock and mourning after fifteen victims die and others on the bus are injured.

A GoFundMe campaign is set up to help the victims' families, which surpasses $8.5 million, five days after the crash. Donations pour in from across Canada, the United States and across the world. This tragic news has touched the hearts of families in sixty-five countries, who have children in team sports.

Students are encouraged to wear hockey jerseys to show support for Humboldt on Jersey Day, six days after the crash. Those who do not have jerseys can wear the team colours of green and gold.

More local news includes a $5.4 million investment from the federal government to expand Summerside's dairy processing plant. Amalgamated Dairies Ltd (ADL) is a cooperative and is owned by 165 family dairy farms on Prince Edward Island. We are happy to know that, when we buy milk, we are supporting local farmers. This investment and expansion will bring much-needed local jobs to town, so it is the talk of the community.

Midway through the second week of April, we have a beautiful spring day. The sun shines brightly in a cloudless sky and the temperature climbs to a high of 5°C. We enjoy a walk on the boardwalk and see lots of others out doing the same. The wind remains cold and I'm glad of a hat. The harbour is full of mini bergs from the ice that is breaking up in the Strait, as it is pushed in by the tide. We hear birds singing, but there are no other obvious signs of spring.

***

I'm up before dawn on a Tuesday morning as I'm going to work. I see the sky change as the sun starts to rise. A low mist hangs over the bay, which appears in muted shades of grey-blue. To the east, the sky is tinged with pink. The cloudless sky means it is another cold morning, although the forecast is for 3°C later this afternoon. For now, it is still below freezing.

I've been working at the convenience store for two weeks now and I'm slowly getting used to the routine of these early morning starts. There is something quite brutal about starting work at 5.45. It is not that I haven't worked shifts before, or even worked throughout the night, but it just feels like such an unsocial time of day to be up and busy when most people are still asleep.

***

It is my birthday during the second week of April and we are travelling to Charlottetown, as I have a hair appointment. We wake to large flakes of wet snow, which soon changes to rain. The sky is overcast and gloomy and a complete contrast to the sunshine of two days ago.

We arrive in Charlottetown, too early for my appointment, so we head to Tim Hortons where we treat ourselves to breakfast wraps. Although we ate before we left home, the taste of a savoury bacon and egg breakfast wrap is too tempting, especially since we haven't eaten bacon in more than a month, since we started our healthy eating plan. We enjoy our wraps and linger over our tea/coffee. It makes a change not to be rushing and to have time to sit and people-watch for a few minutes.

My hair appointment takes much longer than anticipated (more than three hours!) and poor Mr Candytuft is hanging around waiting for me – first in the salon, until he hears that I will be a further hour (this announced by me with a head full of foils and wrapped in a towel) – then wandering the streets. I find him waiting in the car when I finally escape the salon. My hair looks great, though I'm not sure he thinks it was worth the wait. I feel guilty for keeping him waiting, so I tell him I will buy lunch.

We try an Indian restaurant first, on a recommendation from my stylist, but are unimpressed when the waitress asks us to move to a tiny table, almost on top of another couple. There isn't even elbow room and I feel like part of their conversation. We get up and leave and decide to head to our favourite pub instead.

The Churchill Arms is an authentic British pub – such pubs are a rarity in Canada. We first discovered it on a day trip to Prince Edward Island years ago. It has the appearance and atmosphere of a proper pub, with bulldogs adorning the bar area. The walls are full of Churchill memorabilia and famous quotes from his speeches.

We enter the warm and cosy pub after a cold and windy walk from our car. I can hardly believe that it is mid-April and yet I'm still wearing a winter coat and boots. We find a table above the bar area, which gives us a vantage point for observing the room.

The server takes our order – hot tea for a cold day and traditional British fare – steak and kidney pie and chips for Mr Candytuft, whilst I decide on chicken tikka masala, served with rice and naan bread. The food is absolutely delicious – Mr Candytuft decides he likes curried chips and dips them in my curry sauce. Neither of us has room for dessert, though we notice that they have deep-fried Mars bars on the menu (we've never actually tried them, but know that they are considered something of a delicacy in Scotland), as well as their version of a 99. I haven't seen 99s since the days of Mr Whippy's ice-cream vans

– for those of you who lack an English upbringing, a 99 is an ice-cream cornet topped with a Cadbury's Flake chocolate bar. I've done something similar at home from time to time, but I have never seen them on a Canadian menu. If you ever find yourself in Charlottetown, you have to try this pub – and I have it on good authority (Mr Candytuft) that the Guinness is good, too.

Our journey home begins as overcast and windy, but the sun comes out as we approach Summerside. We have a couple of stops to make en route and get out of the car to discover that it is now mild and sunny. This is certainly a day of contrast when it comes to the weather – it must be our island climate.

In the evening, we enjoy chocolate cupcakes with chocolate ganache icing, which I had saved in the freezer since Easter. A birthday isn't complete without cake and a candle – the perfect end to a perfect day.

The next morning, I head out to town for a walk. Mr Candytuft opts to remain at home watching soccer (it is Saturday and there are four matches on television). I set off along the boardwalk, but quickly discover why there are few people about. The wind is bitterly cold and right in my face. It is coming from the north and, although no wind chill was forecast, it is making for extremely unpleasant walking.

I only walk as far as the lighthouse, on an exposed stretch of shore, at which point, I retrace my steps to the car. My initial thought is to drive to the car park further along the shore, but I abandon that idea and head for home instead. There are days when it is wise to admit defeat against the elements and this is one of them.

A few days later, we are out for a morning walk and it is raining. It is not particularly heavy rain – more of an April shower. The day is windy again and it is that piercingly cold wind that seems to have persisted for most of April. The calendar may indicate it is almost the end of the third week of April, but the weather has yet to warm up.

Yesterday, when we were out walking, we passed the

ospreys' nest at the top of the telegraph pole and Mr Candytuft commented that it would not be long until they returned from their winter migration. When we pass the nest this morning, we spot one of the ospreys sitting right on the edge of the nest. There is no sign of the other one, so maybe it is awaiting the return of its mate.

I research ospreys later at home and learn that they do not begin to breed until they are between three and five years old and, in their first year together, an osprey pair will build a nest and establish a territory, then return to breed the following year: osprey pairs generally mate for life.

We head down to the bridge over the stream where we have previously watched the muskrats. The wetland is flooded with melt-water and there is no sign of the muskrats. We pause to watch a couple of ducks dabbling – they look like ballerinas in tutus, as their feet paddle furiously to maintain their position. A little further along, we hear a babbling brook. It is such a soothing sound and one we could listen to all day, except for the fact that it is raining and cold and we want to complete our walk.

We are glad to return to the car and head home to the warmth. As we leave town, the rain stops and the sun appears. The sky clears and it looks like a change of season, but we are not about to be fooled by appearances, as there is snow forecast for tomorrow.

At lunchtime, I set off for the knitting group. It is a month since I last attended and I have missed the social aspect of spending a couple of hours with like-minded individuals, sharing the joy of knitting and chatting about life in general.

Today's topic of conversation is the forthcoming Royal Wedding of Prince Harry and Meghan Markle. We understand that the wedding invitations have been sent, but none of us has been fortunate enough to receive one.

I'm working on a vintage jacket, which I started at the end of January. The project was on hold for a while, as I ran out of a yarn that was discontinued. I finally tracked some down but had to buy it from the United States. I finished the knitting part a couple of weeks ago but had not had time to do the finishing. Today, I start sewing the jacket together. I manage to get the main body stitched but have yet to do the sleeves.

Later at home, my attention turns to my seedlings, which have been outgrowing their pots during the last week or so. I spend an hour repotting sweet peas and pinching off the tops, to encourage more bushy growth. It is likely to be at least another month before I can even consider planting outdoors, as the temperature remains cold and there is still the possibility of frost.

With thoughts of gardening in mind, I am going to a meeting of the local garden club this evening. When I suggested this to Mr Candytuft about a month ago, he agreed to go with me, but now he has decided not to attend. I am almost ready to leave when he changes his mind and says he is coming with me. The idea behind attending this meeting is to meet people and feel more a part of this community. Plus, I'm hoping to be able to buy plants from other members, once the gardening season gets underway.

In the event, we are delayed by traffic and the rainy conditions and arrive after the start of the meeting. There is a presentation about pruning – mainly about trees, though it also features pruning of shrubs and hedges. The presenter is knowledgeable and the talk is very interesting and generates quite a lot of questions.

We leave before the end of the meeting as Mr Candytuft seems anxious to get home, so I don't have a chance to talk to any of the members on this occasion, but I intend to follow up and contact them about joining. They have an open garden scheme, which sees gardens across the district open to visitors over four months of spring and summer and an all-important plant sale next month, where I hope to find some good plants to start our garden.

The next day, I'm in the kitchen sowing seeds in a tray. As I look out of the window, snow is falling. The noise of the wind is audible above the radio. How can I be sowing seeds when the winter weather persists into mid-April?

Yesterday, I noticed that the ice was receding from Malpeque Bay and I could see water for the first time in months, but news reports state that, although the ice had been clearing from the Gulf of Saint Lawrence, those cold north-easterly winds pushed all of the ice up against the north shore of Prince Edward Island and ice-breakers operated by the Canadian Coast Guard are busy trying to clear the pack ice.

It is Monday morning of the last week of April and we are out for a walk by the harbour. The temperature is 6°C: the sky is a brilliant blue and cloudless and there is a feeling that spring is in the air. The boardwalk is busy with walkers and runners, though Mr Candytuft is the only walker in shorts! I'm dressed for cold and I'm glad of my scarf and gloves, as the wind still has an edge to it.

The trees stand in contrast to the sky and have yet to cast off their winter colour of dull brown, but the sap must be starting to rise, as there are buds appearing on the willows and soon the catkins will be budding.

A song sparrow sits at the top of a tree close to the path and is singing a joyous song. We stop to listen, but he seems to have stage-fright and takes off, only to land further along the path and resume his singing.

We pause at the bridge to look for the muskrats but see no sign of them on our way out: on our return, we see one swimming around close to the bank and watch for a while. We see a Downy woodpecker in a tree and crack open a peanut. I place a piece on the handrail a short distance from where we are standing and the woodpecker comes down for it, bunny-hopping along the rail to claim its reward, before flying back to the safety of the tree to eat it. It is a male bird, as he has a distinctive red patch on the back of his head: he is mostly black, with bold white spots on his wings and his striped head is black and white. The Downy is the smallest species of woodpecker in North America and has a short bill, which he uses to make a drumming noise on trees.

We place another piece of peanut on the rail when we see the woodpecker looking for more food, but a Blue Jay swoops in to claim it. This is Prince Edward Island's provincial bird, which is plentiful and visible at the feeders. In the pecking order, Blue Jays will chase smaller birds to get the food first.

Though generally wary of people, this little woodpecker seems quite tame and comes close enough for us to get a good look at his beautiful plumage. Once the Blue Jay is distracted, I place another piece of peanut within reach and the Downy claims it, before we continue our walk.

Both of the osprey nests we spotted last summer are now occupied, so the nesting pairs have returned from their winter migration. Ospreys breed in Canada between April and September and live close to water, as they feed almost exclusively on fish. Their distinctive stick nests are sited on top of telegraph poles. One of the main predators of osprey eggs and chicks is the racoon, which is quite agile and can climb. Building the nest high off the ground, with a clear vantage point, affords some protection from such predators. Ospreys also have the advantage of powerfully sharp talons and a hooked beak for defending their territory.

On our way back through town, we see human activity as gardens are being raked and litter picked up. It feels like spring is finally here and it is time to get ready for the warmer weather.

***

In the absence of being registered with a family physician, we have our first experience of attending our local walk-in clinic. We arrive at 08.30, thirty minutes before the clinic opens, only to find there is already a queue of seven people ahead of us. When the doors open, we wait our turn to register at reception. I tentatively ask how long we can expect to wait (I've brought a book to read) and I'm informed it is likely to be 'a few hours'. At this, we ask if we can leave and go for breakfast and come back later.

We head to Tim Hortons for a cup of tea and a breakfast

wrap, then I suggest we go for our morning walk, but Mr Candytuft thinks it is better not to be gone too long in case the wait is shorter than anticipated. We stop at the library and I get another book to read, as I'm almost finished with my current one.

We arrive back at the walk-in clinic about an hour after we registered. A woman who is ahead of us informs us that no one has been seen yet. I let the receptionist know we are back and we sit down to wait our turn. The wait is a long one. I have finished the first book and read 150 pages of the second one by the time we are called in, almost four hours after our return. Our wait resumes in a patient assessment room. The system in most walk-in clinics I've been to in Canada is one in which the doctor rotates around a series of rooms, rather than the patients all being seen in the doctor's own room. Walk-in patients are fitted in between regular appointments, which is the reason for such long waiting times.

Finally, the doctor appears and we talk to him about the desperate doctor shortage in the province of Prince Edward Island. We emerge from the clinic after 3 p.m. Our-six-and-a-half-hour wait is over. I hadn't anticipated spending almost an entire day waiting to get a prescription.

***

We are on the road before 7 a.m. and approaching the Confederation Bridge, which stretches before us across the Northumberland Strait. It is cloudy and overcast on this morning in late April, but the sight of the spans of the bridge is still impressive. As we cross, we see the Strait is now clear of ice.

We are on our way to Halifax, one of our favourite cities in the Maritimes. This is our first trip to Nova Scotia since we arrived on Prince Edward Island and our first visit to Halifax in over two years.

We stop for breakfast at the Big Stop, not far from the border of Nova Scotia. Mr Candytuft jokes that it feels different being back in Canada! I ask him if he has remembered his passport.

After breakfast, we continue our journey and cross into Nova Scotia two hours after we set off from home. We pass the Wandlyn Inn, which is a well-known safe haven for travellers who become stranded during winter storms. We stayed there once some years ago and heard tales of people being stuck for days and sleeping in hallways because the inn was so overcrowded. Situated on an isthmus between Fort Lawrence, New Brunswick and Amherst, Nova Scotia, the area is subject to major winter storms that often close the highway.

The high point of the road is the Cobequid Pass. We climb hill after hill on our approach. There is a toll, payable at the pass, and we discover it is 'cash only', once we get to the toll booth. In this day of payment by plastic almost everywhere, this comes as a surprise: we have crossed before but had not remembered this. Still, it is only $4.00 and we manage to pay our toll, before continuing through the Cobequid Mountains. As we descend, we catch glimpses of the Bay of Fundy and the sun appears from behind the clouds.

The scenery is still dark evergreens and leafless deciduous trees. Tiny patches of snow linger in sheltered spots. The highway stretches before us and we enjoy some sightseeing, recalling previous visits to this area.

As we get south of Truro, the weather improves – the cloud is higher and the sun is shining. When we stop for a short break, we find that the temperature is mild – around 15°C, as opposed to 5°C at home. Not only that, but the grass is green – ours is still a dead-looking brown.

By the time we reach Halifax, spring has arrived: gardens look green, spring flowers are starting to bloom and the trees are in bud. Pedestrians are walking around wearing tee shirts and shorts and it is 17°C.

I recall that this has happened before. When we lived in Nova Scotia, about two hours east of Halifax, we left home in what felt like late winter and arrived to find Halifax in full bloom.

Mr Candytuft is a man on a mission and heads straight to the bike shop. He has his eye on a couple of bikes and this is his opportunity to try them out and talk about technical specifications with the salesman.

After a while, I drift back to the car and settle down to wait and read my book. It is pleasant in the sunshine and I have the car windows open. I anticipate a lengthy wait, but I'm only on a second chapter when he reappears, saying he has the information he wants, and plans to go home and compare different makes and models before making a final decision.

We head to Costco before setting off for home. We stock up on favourite foods, which are more difficult to find on our island, as well as fresh produce. We have our large cooler with us and lots of ice packs to ensure everything stays cold and fresh during our long drive home.

By the time we reach the Confederation Bridge, the weather is beautiful – the sky is a deep blue with barely a cloud visible and the sunshine is bright. I am driving and, even with sunglasses, the glare is strong.

We reach home – we've been on the road for ten hours and have travelled more than 600 kilometres/370 miles. I vow that I don't plan to do this journey in a day again – we are both so stiff from prolonged sitting that we can barely stand up straight when we get out of the car. It is good to be home.

Saturday morning arrives and with it, April showers. I sleep late after yesterday's long drive to Halifax and when I get up I see a dark sky and rain falling steadily, as it patters on the roof and windows. Mr Candytuft informs me that the forecast is for the rain to continue throughout the coming week.

Spring really has arrived and this is confirmed by our first sighting of a robin in our garden. The sky clears and, although it isn't sunny, the rain stops. I take advantage of the windy conditions and get two loads of laundry washed and out on the line to dry. Finally, it is mild enough to use the washing line! When I bring the laundry in later, it has that wonderful smell that only comes from drying outside.

CHAPTER NINE

MAY: SPRING AT LAST!

The beginning of May sees the grass becoming green and our first really mild day, as the temperature reaches 17°C but the weather continues to be changeable. We have a severe thunderstorm in the evening after the day's mild weather and a cold front moves in, with torrential rain, which continues throughout the night. I toss and turn and listen to the rain pounding on the roof and windows.

I have an appointment in Charlottetown and it is only 4°C as we set off in the car. We drive along wet roads and seek signs of spring, but see little evidence of it so far. After my appointment, we decide to return home, rather than spend time in the cold.

We travel through the community of Hunter River and Mr Candytuft suggests that we go in search of the Mennonite farm. I read about this farm online in an old newspaper article from last summer. I learned that five families of Old Order Mennonites from St Jacobs, Ontario relocated to Prince Edward Island in the summer of 2017, because of the lack of affordable farms in Ontario. The couple who purchased the farm, which we plan to visit, opened a farm shop selling organic eggs, home-baked goods and seasonal organic vegetables and grass-fed beef. We have a rough idea of where the farm is located, but trust to the fact that there will be a sign for their shop. We know we are on the right road once we see a yellow horse and buggy caution sign at the side of the road, which warns motorists to watch for horse-drawn carriages and to share the road. The distinctive black horse-drawn carriages have started appearing on the Island's roads as families settle in the area.

We find the farm, which is perfectly situated along a drive of birch trees (still bare after winter) and with a pond in front of the heritage farmhouse. We park in the farmyard and get out of the car. We see a trailer in the yard, which is full of plants and, whilst we are looking at these, the farmer's wife appears and greets us. She is dressed plainly in a long black dress with an apron and a cap.

Mennonites have a strong devotion to the land and shun many modern conveniences, though they do use electricity. Their primary method of transportation is their covered horse-drawn buggy. They do not drive cars but can ride in them as passengers. I later learn that the house they bought has an in-law suite, which they use for the commercial side of their business, including their baking.

We are invited to look inside their greenhouse, which is full of thriving plants. It is still too early in the season to buy anything, as we don't own a greenhouse and the danger of frost can persist until late May.

We are then shown into the house through the customer entrance and find an array of baked goods for sale. The pies look delicious – a rhubarb one catches my eye – but we resist, as we are still on our healthy eating plan. We buy two dozen fresh, organic eggs and chat about the beef they produce. We learn that it is currently out of stock, but they will have a fresh supply for sale later in the month. I suspect that Mr Candytuft will be keen to sample some.

On retracing our steps to the highway, we decide to stop at a bakery/cafe, which we passed earlier. I had suggested we try it some weeks earlier, but Mr Candytuft had been reluctant to try somewhere new. Today, however, he agrees to take the plunge and eat here. He quickly feels at home and is pleased to discover that they have his favourite meal on their menu – all-day breakfast. He tucks into his breakfast and I try their homemade soup. The cafe has a cosy atmosphere and seems to be frequented by locals, at least at this time of the year, though I imagine it will be a popular tourist spot in summer. We finish our lunch and head for home. It has been an interesting day and we have discovered two new places we intend to visit again soon.

After seeing so many baked goods for sale during our recent trip out, I decide it is time for a little treat and set to work in the kitchen. I bake raspberry scones, which are a favourite of mine. Mr Candytuft keeps saying not to tempt him with scones (though I have a batch of sultana scones in the freezer – just in case), so I make him some healthy treats. The first of these is a healthier version of a chocolate chip cookie, which is made with coconut oil, rather than butter, and with very little sugar. This is a hit with him and he promptly eats three! I point out that they are only 'healthier' if eaten in moderation. (I hide the rest of the batch in the freezer.)

The other healthy recipe I decide to try is for Bakewell tart balls. These sweet treats are made with Medjool dates, almonds, sultanas and cranberries. They are flavoured with vanilla extract and almond essence and they have that marzipan-like stickiness, as well as tasting like Bakewell tart. They are a breeze to make, as all I have to do is pit the dates, cut them up, then throw the whole lot into my food processor. Once blitzed, I simply roll them into balls and place them in the fridge for thirty minutes to set. We both adore these and I know I will soon be stocking up on the necessary ingredients for another batch.

***

After last month's garden club meeting, I spent a couple of weeks trying to contact someone for further information about membership. I eventually managed to speak to a lady, who told me about their next planned event and suggested we attend and join on the night. We are going to one of the local garden centres for a garden club evening. We manage to arrive early, to discover that everyone else is even earlier and the car park is already full. We find a space and enter the greenhouse and I wander around until I see someone who looks official – a lady with a clipboard – I approach her and ask about membership and she is only too happy to take our money and issue membership cards.

The evening is a chance for garden club members to buy plants at discount prices and some of them are certainly taking full advantage of this. We choose a small collection of perennials and a few herbs, and join the queue behind a lady with a double-decker cart that is absolutely heaving with plants.

We are starting a garden from scratch, with nothing more than a holly bush in it so far (and it isn't looking like it survived the winter). Although I planted a lot of bulbs last autumn, they have not appeared, apart from the ones that were pushed out of the ground by the frost and have rotted in the wet conditions. This is a huge disappointment as I had been hoping to have some spring colour with sunny yellow daffodils, crocus and a selection of smaller flowering bulbs to enjoy. As I've seen bulbs up in other gardens, some of which are already flowering, it isn't looking very promising.

My ambitious plans for an English-style cottage garden started when I sowed hollyhocks from seed last summer and planted out the seedlings in the autumn. I have yet to see a sign of a hollyhock leaf, so they may not have survived the winter. In keeping with this plan, I have chosen Sweet Woodruff, Irish moss, Sedum 'Autumn Joy', which is a favourite of mine, and *Campanula persicifolia*, also known as fairy bellflower, which has been traditionally grown in cottage gardens for generations. I also buy some herbs with which to start a herb garden.

The garden club has a plant sale later in May, at which I hope to add to my plant collection. In the meantime, I'm still growing seedlings at home and have tomatoes in pots, sweet peas taking over the living room and annual flowers in seed trays. Until the danger of frost has passed, all must remain indoors, and they have now been joined by my new purchases, although these will be placed outdoors during the daytime.

***

I am outside doing battle with the laundry on a cold and extremely windy morning. By the time I have two loads of washing on the line to dry; I feel half-frozen and scurry inside to warm up with a cup of tea. It is several weeks since I last chatted to my friend in Norway – working has made keeping up with everyday activities more difficult and limited my free time. I'm pouring the tea when she calls me and I disappear into my sewing room for a girly chat. It is good to catch up and to feel a little less isolated.

We are both displaced to countries other than those we grew up in, but I consider myself lucky that, for the most part, I don't have to understand another language (though I do work in a French community, the customers speak English). We chat for an hour about life in general and knitting in particular. She is learning to knit socks, which have long been on my 'to do' list and I'm interested to hear about her progress.

By the time we finish our conversation, the laundry, which has been on the line for less than two hours, is dry. It is so windy that I'm lucky it is still on the line. I take it in and hang out a third load before we go into town on a few errands. It is one of those days when I can't get warm and I'm back in my winter jacket, even though we are almost a third of the way through May. I feel lazy for not wanting to go for a walk, but I can't face that bitingly cold wind in my face. As soon as we have finished our errands, we return home to the warmth of central heating and hot tea.

***

The American goldfinches have returned from their winter migration. We last saw them in our garden in late October. These yellow and black canary-like birds are known for their bright plumage and distinctive tweets. Their migration is somewhat irregular, as some remain in Canada if they have a good supply of food. Those that remain are not as easy to identify in winter due to the fact that their plumage changes to a more subtle brown. I'm fairly certain ours migrated, as I haven't seen any small birds in the garden since before the winter and it is a delight to see them flitting across the garden, as they dart in and out of the trees.

There are daffodils blooming in our neighbour's garden, but still no sign of the bulbs we planted last autumn. I clear the rotting bulbs from the surface of the garden, feeling somewhat dispirited that the anticipated springtime display has come to nothing.

***

We go for a walk one Sunday afternoon in mid-May. It is more of an afternoon stroll than vigorous exercise. There is shelter amongst the trees, for which we are grateful, as it is only 10°C and there is a cold wind coming from the east. The sky is sunny and blue, and there is the smell of pine as we walk through the woods, mixed with the smell of seaweed on the shore. The tide is on its way out and it will be low tide in three hours. The harbour has a mixed semidiurnal tide, with two high and two low tides per day, which differ in height.

Pausing on the bridge over the wetland area, we feed a young woodpecker, which comes down for almonds. An older male appears, with the distinctive red spot on the back of his head, but he seems nervous today, as the boardwalk is noisy and busy with families enjoying their Sunday afternoon. Below the bridge, we spot yellow flowers along the banks of the stream, which I later discover are wild yellow violets. They have large heart-shaped leaves and are covered in pretty flowers. Protected from the cold winds in this sheltered place, they still get the benefit of the sun's rays encouraging them to open. They must still be quite hardy though, as it there hasn't been a sustained period of mild weather to encourage spring to burst forth.

I'm leaving for work the following morning as the sun is coming up at 5.30. The sky is pink and the horizon is a smudge of deep blue with a light mist on the water. Wispy clouds are high in the sky and there is a vapour trail from an aircraft higher still. The whole scene is breathtaking and so peaceful. I glance back at the scene as we head west along the highway, reluctant to miss a moment of this perfect sunrise. Mr Candytuft is taking me to work, as he wants the use of the car today.

I am reminded that this coming weekend is a holiday. Victoria Day is a public holiday, which is celebrated on the Monday preceding the 25 May, in honour of Queen Victoria's birthday (24 May). It always strikes me as somewhat archaic to be marking this event, especially as there is no such holiday in the UK.

Victoria Day was declared a Canadian holiday in 1845 and officially named following Queen Victoria's death in 1901. The day is marked in most places with parades and fireworks, and the weekend is considered by most to mark the start of summer. Considering the fact that spring has barely got underway, there are no leaves on the trees, and the temperatures are still on the cool side, this seems a little premature. Having said this, it is of greater concern to me that we are only five weeks from the summer solstice after which, the daylight hours begin to shorten once again.

Later in the week, a change in my work schedule provides an unexpected day off and the chance to go for a walk on the boardwalk. It is only two days since we were last down here, but the change is dramatic. The trees are bursting into bud and everything looks more verdant.

Although it is a weekday, there are lots of people out enjoying the sunshine. I start my walk in a spring jacket but have to remove it as, once we reach the shelter of the trees and we are out of the wind, the sun feels hot on my back. Everyone has a spring in their step and it feels like spring is really here.

There is a new addition to the birdhouses, partly hidden in the trees. This exclusive barn feeder has a sign stating 'members only' and the front is covered in tasty birdseed and peanut treats. I love the fact that the community takes ownership of this space and the wildlife that lives here, not only providing feeders but ensuring a healthy supply of food for the birds, red squirrels and chipmunks.

We stop to make friends with a dog called Rosie, who is a Shih Tzu/Poodle cross. She is pleased to meet us and we have an interesting chat with her owner. People are happy to stop and chat for a while, now the weather has improved. I've been feeling under the weather since late last week, with a lingering virus, so it is good to be out enjoying the fresh air and it certainly lifts my mood.

When we return home, I discover that it is 20°C and the warmest day this year. It is mid-May, so high time for an improvement in the weather. I have laundry drying on the line when the weather changes suddenly and I see the first big drops of rain hitting the windows. I rush outside to take the laundry indoors and manage to get the last of it in before the heavens open and we have torrential rain. The cloud base is low and it looks misty over the bay: typical maritime weather. Oh well, at least we enjoyed the best of the day.

We spend a rainy afternoon watching the film version of *Paddington*, which I found at the library. It is hilarious and very enjoyable. I cannot remember the last time I laughed as much and I can't wait to see *Paddington 2*. I won't spoil it for those of you who haven't had the pleasure, but I highly recommend it. There are some memorable moments, which stay with me long after the film is over.

As we approach Victoria Day weekend, the weather continues to be cool and windy, with night-time frosts. I'm relieved that I delayed planting any of my seedlings outdoors and that the perennials, which I bought at the garden club event at a local garden centre, remain in our living room. I talk to a neighbour, who is preparing his vegetable garden for planting. He tells me he won't be sowing any of his seeds until June, due to the continuing risk of frost

I had researched this area and discovered that it is in frost hardiness zone 5B. The last frost date is supposed to be between 21 and 30 April, so we are already a month behind this year. Considering that our first frost date is between 1 and 10 October, we have a very short growing season.

Victoria Day weekend arrives, which is the time when Canadian gardeners typically plant their gardens for summer, but there will be no planting in our garden this weekend, as the temperatures remain unsettled. Saturday is cold, wet and windy but, as I'm working, I won't be too worried to be missing any planting opportunities.

Saturday is also the Royal wedding of Prince Harry and Meghan Markle, soon to be known as the Duke and Duchess of Sussex. With the four-hour time difference, television coverage of the event starts early, but I don't worry about the preliminary build-up to the actual wedding. By the time I turn on the television, most of the guests are already in their seats at St George's Chapel, Windsor,

Mr Candytuft, who is definitely not a royalist, keeps throwing in comments and complaining about it being on at all until I point out that he wouldn't be happy if I talked all the way through the F.A. Cup Final, which is on later this afternoon. After this, he gets bored and wanders off, leaving me to watch it in peace. As I have to go to work later, there will be no celebratory tea party, complete with bunting (which I made for the Queen's Diamond Jubilee in 2012), this afternoon. Today, I settle for some home-baked scones and a cup of Yorkshire Gold, both of which Mr Candytuft devours with relish.

I'm back at work on Sunday morning, which gets off to another cool start, although the mercury climbs to 17°C and people are in a holiday mood. Finally, the sun is shining and it feels like a good day for an ice cream. Mr Candytuft shows up during my shift. He has been out for a bike ride and comes in looking rather overheated. He buys a Magnum Double Caramel and stays long enough to finish it before pedalling off towards home.

Later in the evening, Mr Candytuft reports that he has some symptoms of concern, which necessitate a trip to the Emergency Department of our local hospital. This is our second experience of health care in the province in almost as many weeks. This time, we arrive to find a packed waiting area and a receptionist, who sends us to the triage nurse. After registering at reception, we wait for triage before the nurse informs us that there is a three- to four-hour waiting time: at least this is shorter than the waiting time on our last visit to the walk-in clinic.

Mr Candytuft tells me to go home, as I've been working all day and he will call me when he needs collecting. I go home, but cannot settle; clock-watching until 10.30 p.m. I'm desperately tired and want my bed, but I know that I have to go out again. I decide to head back to the hospital and find out what is happening.

I arrive to find he is no longer in the waiting area. Upon inquiry, I'm informed that the doctor is seeing him now and to take a seat. The place is locked up and there is no entry without permission, even as his next-of-kin.

I sit in the waiting area and eventually, Mr Candytuft appears. He is to have further investigations within the next week or so but, for now, he has been discharged. We return home, where Mr Candytuft devours everything he can lay his hands on, as he has hardly eaten all day and I fall, thankfully, into bed.

Monday is Victoria Day and, as I have the day off, we decide to go for a walk. Mr Candytuft wants to go out on his bike, so we agree to meet in town and walk together. The sun is shining in an almost cloudless blue sky. There is a youth triathlon on the trail and lots of people are out enjoying the sunshine.

We see a chipmunk, which runs up to us looking for a treat but is disappointed as we don't have any nuts with us today. We haven't seen any chipmunks around since last autumn.

Although chipmunks are small rodents, they are very cute. They are only about 16–30 centimetres/6-8 inches in length, with their distinctive black and white stripes, large eyes and bushy tails. Their chubby cheeks can pouch an incredible amount of food, as they can stash up to three times the size of their head. I have fond memories of feeding a tame chipmunk some years ago, which came right up to us and took large quantities of peanuts.

Further research reveals that chipmunks sleep for up to fifteen hours a day (what a life!) and they are members of the squirrel family. Their stomping grounds range from Canada to Mexico, and they tend to live in underground burrows. They hibernate over winter, so this explains their long absence.

The trees are changing and their leaves are starting to bud. We see fiddlehead ferns in the wood. Fiddleheads are considered something of a delicacy in Canada and are harvested for use as a vegetable. They are served cooked and are nutritional powerhouses, full of antioxidants, fibre and Omega-3 fatty acids. I've only eaten them once: they were served at a meal with friends and I enjoyed them. For some reason, I have never actually tried preparing them myself.

After our walk, Mr Candytuft heads back on his bike, whilst I drive home from town. I'm heading towards Summerside airport, which is located on a former military base when a four-engine turbo-prop Hercules military transport aircraft flies directly overhead. He is so low that the shadow of the aircraft passes right over the car.

There are two Hercules that are regular visitors to Summerside. They come on training and search and rescue exercises. A couple of weeks ago, they were night flying and I was awoken by their engine noise at 2 a.m. as they were taking off. Their engines make a deep rumbling noise, which is especially loud in the middle of the night.

I took advantage of the mild weather and put my perennials outside on the back deck before going out for our walk, along with the three largest tomato plants, which I started from seed.

The afternoon was warm, with the temperature climbing to 20°C, but I failed to take the coastal wind into consideration. When I go out to collect them around 5.30 p.m., I discover that the three tomatoes are wilting: their leaves and lower branches are limp. It may be 20°C, but they needed protection from that wind and I will be lucky if they survive.

***

I am three weeks late filing our tax returns, but there will be no financial penalty: Revenue Canada only penalise those who owe money for filing late returns. It has taken weeks to sort out the details of the return and make sense of them and this required specialist help. I'm glad to have this out of the way for another year.

My reward is an afternoon curled up on the sofa watching *Paddington 2* and Mr Candytuft joins me. The sequel is as enjoyable as the original. It is lovely to spend some time together and forget the outside world, where yet another storm is blowing in and torrential rain is pounding against the windows. There are days when the best place to be is at home and this is one of them.

The next morning, there is a heavy frost on the rooftops and the car windscreen requires scraping before I can drive to work. It is a very cold start to the day. On my return home later, I notice our neighbours have erected a flagpole. I joke that now we will know when they are in residence.

The last weekend of May is the garden club's perennial plant sale, which is an outdoor event. We go down to buy some plants for our garden. It may be 10°C, but the wind is making it feel much colder and we are not outside for long before we are both feeling the effects. The garden club members are friendly and we chat to some of them and are invited to visit their gardens at any time. We make our purchases and are relieved to return home. Once we get there and unload the plants, I realise I cannot identify some of them (they are unlabelled), so we go back to ask the experts after I fail to identify them from my gardening books.

Thankfully, the plants have all been kept outdoors, so they don't need to be hardened off, which is a relief, as my living room contains a lot of plants and seedlings; all waiting to go outside if ever the weather warms up.

I spend some time in the afternoon baking an apple crumble with the last of the Cortland apples from the freezer. They stored well and the crumble is delicious with hot custard: the perfect treat on a cold Saturday.

After investing in some new gardening tools, Mr Candytuft decides to go out into the garden and clear what looks like an old vegetable patch. He seeks my advice regarding the location of some rhubarb, which we spotted last summer, but has mysteriously disappeared. He gets to work digging the bed and I decide that the wisest course of action is to retreat indoors out of the way. Some two hours later, he reappears, saying he found the whole process of digging surprisingly satisfying (who would have thought he would become a keen gardener?). He has cleared about half of the bed. Soon after he has showered and changed, he is asleep on the sofa. It seems that digging is harder than he thought.

Our garden may still be in the planning stage, but an unexpected message from the gardening club announces that there are free plants up for grabs on a first come, first served basis. As they are Sedum 'Autumn Joy', which is a favourite of mine, I send Mr Candytuft on a mission to collect some, as I'm working and cannot go myself. His mission is a success and we now have two large sedum plants to add to our garden.

Back in the kitchen, I bake potato scones and make a carrot soup for lunch on what is yet another cold day. Mr Candytuft is busy again clearing the vegetable garden and comes in to tell me that it was last used six years ago. He has been chatting to some of the maintenance crew, who were busy cutting the grass and one of them told him that it was a beautiful vegetable garden with flourishing crops. At least we now know it is worth the effort involved in clearing it, as it can be productive again.

The following day, we have to clear up the waste material

from the garden. It is the end of May and it is starting to feel like summer is approaching. The temperature is 25°C, as the weather is coming from the south, bringing a day of glorious sunshine.

In the afternoon, I go to the knitting group to seek help with my current knitting project. The vintage jacket, which I have been knitting, has a crochet picot edging and I don't crochet. I'm fortunate to find someone in the shop who not only crochets but is willing to give me a crash-course. Within about twenty minutes, I've grasped the concept and I'm ready to try the edging on my own. After an hour of concentration, my brain feels overloaded and I lay my work aside and head home.

CHAPTER TEN

JUNE: RETURN TO GREEN GABLES

As a second hot day forecast, the first day of June sees us heading out to do some exploring. Since we last visited Green Gables Heritage Place at the end of December, when it was snow-covered, I am keen to make a return visit. We decide to do the tour of historic sites and head towards Cavendish. As we drive along the route, after leaving the main highway, I comment that we might see a bald eagle. We round a corner and there is an eagle right in front of us, soaring over the river, but the best is yet to come.

We continue a bit further when we see a sight that takes our breath away. There are six bald eagles circling overhead. We have never seen a group like this before and pull off the road for a better look. We watch as they continue to circle: maybe they are watching some potential prey but, whatever the reason for their behaviour; they are a spectacle that we will never forget.

With a chocolate-brown body, white head and tail, large yellow beak and a wingspan of more than six feet, the bald eagle is a very distinctive bird. I had a close encounter with an eagle a few years ago when one flew right over my head. It couldn't have been more than ten feet above me and it took my breath away with its sheer size.

I later read of the symbolism of the appearance of a bald eagle and learn that when an eagle appears, you are on notice to be courageous and stretch your limits: to reach higher and become more than you believe you are capable of. I have yet to discover the meaning of the appearance of six bald eagles together, but it sounds like I should be soaring high beyond the limits of my imagination.

The first stop on our trip is the birthplace of Lucy Maud Montgomery, the author of *Anne of Green Gables* and the other books in the series. The house is situated in New London, known as 'Clifton' in the Anne books. We arrive to find other tourists already visiting but, as it is still early in the season, it is not crowded. The pretty village of New London overlooks the harbour and the sand dunes, which Lucy would later write about in her books.

Opposite the house, there is a pretty century home with yellow siding and a green roof and a porch with two tempting rocking chairs. I imagine that the owners sit out there and see the world go by – quite literally. The Anne of Green Gables series of novels are hugely popular, especially in Japan. Bus tours of Japanese tourists descend on this part of Prince Edward Island every summer on a pilgrimage to visit the places that are familiar to them from reading the books.

Lucy Maud Montgomery was born on 30 November 1874. The little white house is of clapboard with a traditional shingled roof and a white picket fence. Behind the house, there is a green pump to draw water from the well.

At the front of the house, a brass plaque commemorates the fact that this is Lucy Maud Montgomery's birthplace and there is a blue plaque designating this site as a Canadian Heritage Place. We enter the house through the front door and step into the hall, which is lined with books and souvenirs relating to Lucy Maud. Turning left, we enter the parlour where an introductory talk is already in progress.

Mr Candytuft isn't a fan of guided tours so, once the group moves on, we ask if we can walk through the house and skip the potted history, which is included in many of the exhibits. The downstairs rooms are filled with scrapbooks depicting Lucy's life as a student at Prince of Wales College, Charlottetown and her later years as a writer and teacher.

The house is tiny and there is little room to move, as everyone crowds in to look at the exhibits. The rooms are quite dark and furnished for the period. A steep, narrow staircase leads to the upper storey, where there is a room furnished with a single bed, adorned with a white hand-stitched quilt. The quilt was made in 1916 by the New London Women's Institute, to raise money for the war effort. Each person who contributed ten cents had their name embroidered on the quilt.

The main bedroom is furnished with a rocking cradle and a rag rug. Lucy Maud was born in this room to Hugh John Montgomery and Clara Woolner MacNeill. Her mother's health was not good, so Lucy Maud went to live at the MacNeill homestead in Cavendish, at the home of her maternal grandparents. She remained with them until her marriage to the Reverend Ewan MacDonald in Park Corner (known as Silver Bush in her novels), on 5 July 1911.

Although the tiny rooms under the eaves of the house look quite cosy and inviting, I cannot imagine living here and surviving a Canadian winter without any form of heat. Downstairs in the kitchen, there is a Franklin stove, made of cast-iron, with a kettle on the hob, all ready for a cup of tea. On the wall of the living room, there is a photograph of Lucy Maud, in which she is seen writing at her desk. I wonder what she would have thought, had she known that tourists from all over the world would make the pilgrimage to visit the places associated with her stories.

Our journey continues as we drive into Cavendish to visit Green Gables Heritage Place. At the time of our visit, major construction is underway, so our approach is very different to the quiet scene that greeted us last December.

We park and walk up to the entrance. Mr Candytuft decides

he doesn't want to view another house and opts to wait for me. I head up past the barn and across the farmyard and approach Green Gables. Today, there are quite a lot of visitors around the house, including a school party enjoying their lunch on the lawn.

I enter the house through the front door and step into the parlour beyond the hall. Again, the rooms are quite dark, but this is in keeping with the period. I talk to a guide who informs me that, like many homes in this part of the world, the home started off as a basic one-room house with a loft and was added to over the years, until it resembled the home we see today.

I pass through the dining room and view Matthew's bedroom, which is simply furnished with a bed and wash-stand. I recall from the story that he slept on the ground floor and rarely went upstairs. The tour continues past the dairy porch, pantry and back porch into the kitchen with its old-fashioned cast-iron Waterloo stove, which was used for cooking and heating. It has pride of place in the centre of the room.

The upstairs rooms have been restored and decorated in the style of the late 1800s, as described by Lucy Maud Montgomery in her novels. The room everyone has come to see is, of course, Anne's room, with its white cast-iron bed and her dress hanging on the door. I can imagine her running upstairs from the garden with her red pigtails flying behind her.

Marilla's room is down the hall, along with her sewing room, which contains her sewing machine and a knitting swift (used for winding yarn skeins into balls).

I speak to another guide before leaving the house and tell her about my visit in December. I say that I imagine the house will be much more crowded in a few weeks: she tells me they had 250,000 visitors between May and October 2017. Visitors to the site come from all over the world and we see cars from across Canada and the United States in the parking area.

Stepping out of the house and into the heat of the day, I decide to forgo the trails and look for Mr Candytuft. We were told at the admission gate that it is possible to explore the grounds after closing and plan to do so another time when the trails are less crowded.

We move on and drive into North Rustico for lunch, returning to the restaurant we visited in December. As it is Friday, the lunchtime special is fish and chips, which we both decide to order – so much for healthy eating – and it's absolutely delicious.

Feeling revived and refreshed after lunch, we set forth to explore further. Mr Candytuft is always keen to go down mystery tracks and see where we end up. We find a secret place that is probably missed by the thousands of tourists who flock to Green Gables in the summer. At the end of this track, we find a place called the Swimming Rock. We park the car and walk towards the shore, where we discover a little sand beach, with the red sandstone typical of Prince Edward Island. The land was purchased by the Sterling Women's Institute in 1963 and is now a picnic place, with benches and a little shelter. It is very peaceful as we are the only people here. The water is flat-calm and reflects the almost cloudless blue sky.

We drive on but pause at a scenic lookout to admire the view. A bus tour of Japanese tourists has also stopped for a photo opportunity and they are all busy with their cameras and phones. The scene is one of the most painted panoramas of Prince Edward Island: the tiny community of French River with its brightly painted buildings, overlooking New London Bay.

After continuing our drive along the Green Gables' shore, we arrive at the Green Gables Museum, ahead of the Japanese tour, although only just. We walk in the grounds and take some photos. We approach the museum entrance to find it is crowded with tourists and decide we have had enough cultural heritage for one day. It is hot and humid and our energy is being drained rapidly.

Seeking shelter on the veranda of the gift shop, we sit on a bench in the shade, enjoying a few minutes of peace. I can hardly believe the change in the weather: I was wearing a winter coat a few days ago. Now, even in a summer dress and sandals, I am thankful for the shade.

After a short respite from the heat, we enter the gift shop and browse the shelves. The lady behind the counter asks where we have come from and seems surprised that we live fairly locally, but our accents give us away as not being native Islanders. We chat about the places where we have lived and the differences between city and country living.

Mr Candytuft spots a sweet print on the wall depicting Anne and her bosom friend, Diana, walking hand-in-hand along a typical red-sand Prince Edward Island beach. The print is entitled, 'Kindred Spirits' and I decide to buy two – one to keep and one for my own dear friend, who lives in Norway. Growing up in the United States, she is a huge fan of Anne and I know the print will delight her.

Feeling in need of some fresh air and exercise, we drive to our favourite beach, which we first discovered last September. We drive along the dirt road, well off the beaten track and off the tourist trail. We find many cars parked at the end of the road. On this glorious day, lots of people are enjoying the beach, but it doesn't look crowded because it is such a vast stretch of red sand.

Most people opt to stay close to the beach access and sunbathe, but we walk down to the waterline and along the shore. We paddle and the water is very cold – this north shore is on the Gulf of Saint Lawrence and it is not that long since the ice melted. The waters have not had much time to warm up and never get as warm as the shallower waters of the Northumberland Strait to the south.

We walk quite a long stretch of beach but lose track of time, as neither of us chooses to wear a watch on days like this. When we have walked long enough, we turn and retrace our steps, arriving back at the car with sand between our toes and in need of refreshment (fortunately, we have water in a cooler).

As we head home, we admire the changing scenery – fields

full of dandelions and fresh green leaves on the trees, which are in sharp contrast to the darker green of the conifers.

It has been a wonderful day and the weather has been absolutely perfect. Once we leave the shore, we find it is much hotter and more humid inland. We arrive home feeling a little overheated, as though we have had too much sun, despite sunhats on the beach, and are grateful for a reviving cup of tea.

There is an abrupt end to the hot weather with heavy rain overnight, which continues throughout the morning. A cold front arrives from the north-east, bringing cold winds sweeping across the province, accompanied by driving rain. Temperatures drop to 8°C, but it feels like a wintry 3°C due to the wind chill. As it says on the forecast, 'Mother Nature can't seem to pick a season over Atlantic Canada.'

Yesterday's summer-like heat broke records in the Maritimes for the end of May, but a brutal temperature change sees temperatures dropping by 20°C from Friday's high, with torrential rain. We get off lightly; as yet another snow storm is forecast for Newfoundland.

An overnight frost sees temperatures more associated with late winter than early June. I'm forced to wear my winter coat because of the biting winds and I'm glad to return to the warmth indoors. The heating is back on after a respite of only two days. It is beginning to look like we are not going to be able to turn it off any time soon, as the forecast for the coming week is much the same.

Frosts continue and people in the community are talking about the damage to strawberry and vegetable crops. A heavy frost on Sunday night damaged the early strawberry plants, which were already flowering: the blossom of the strawberry plant becomes the fruit and it can be severely damaged by frost. Fortunately, mid- and late-season berries will not be affected, as they are not yet in flower.

We have to go into Charlottetown and the scenery looks very different on this trip, despite the overcast sky: we see green fields and most of the trees are now in leaf – a few stragglers are only starting to bud, but most have their summer canopy. Wet roads suggest heavy rain earlier in the morning, but we see no sign of it, although there are ominous dark clouds. It is now two months since our last trip to Charlottetown, but we have no wish to linger today, due to the cold. We complete our shopping and return home as soon as possible.

Yet another dull Sunday afternoon finds me in the kitchen and doing some baking. I bake a lemon drizzle cake, which is not part of our healthy eating plan (which we have been following for four months now), but a treat is necessary on days like this and it is delicious with a cup of tea.

I call my mum and catch up on the week's news. She tells me about their hot spring and how well everything is growing and I tell her we haven't even started planting a vegetable garden because of the continuing frosts (we have another frost warning for tonight and we are a third of the way through June). I only managed to put most of my seedlings outside yesterday and was relieved to see they had survived the night. I've been trying to harden them off for a couple of weeks, but some days have been so cold that I've kept them indoors.

***

It is a Thursday afternoon in mid-June and I've been to my knitting group. I recently finished my vintage jacket and took it along for the other knitters to see. They were all impressed by my knitting skills and thought I had finished the jacket quickly: I disagreed because I started it at the end of January. As many of them are inexperienced knitters, their knitting abilities only extend to simple scarves and cowls, therefore, anyone who can knit an entire garment in less than six months is a fast knitter. I came home early because I didn't have a current project to work on, though I did stay long enough to assist a fellow knitter to correct some mistakes in her work.

Today, I dressed in jeans, boots and my winter waterproof jacket because it is so cold again. Now I'm at home, the rain is torrential and streaming down the windows and I'm glad to be indoors. If I had stayed until the end of the knitting group, I would still have been driving home. This morning, we had rain mixed with hail. I keep saying this, but it doesn't feel like June. The weather feels more like winter than late spring.

Every time we have made plans to go anywhere recently, they have been postponed due to the weather. At this rate, the calendar will roll around to the end of our year on Prince Edward Island and we won't have been very far or seen much. The season is short for visiting attractions, as many don't open until mid-June and they close in early September.

I retreat to the kitchen, deciding that a day like today calls for afternoon tea. I bake two double batches of scones – one of sultana, the other raspberry – with the intention of putting most of them in the freezer, to be enjoyed at a later date. I make a pot of Yorkshire Gold and we enjoy tea and scones – Mr Candytuft eats three, after saying only last week that I shouldn't be giving him scones, as he is trying to lose weight!

The torrential rain continues pounding on the roof and windows, but it is cosy in our world: the lamps are lit and we are nice and toasty indoors after my baking session.

A couple of days later we are back in the garden trying to clear an area of ground at the front of the house for a flower bed. This process continues throughout the week, with little progress being made, due to the inclement weather.

It is Saturday morning when Mr Candytuft goes to Charlottetown, allowing me some time on my own. I go for a long walk and enjoy the fresh air and the exercise. Later, I bake a loaf of French bread and whilst that is baking, I take advantage of some free time to get my sewing machine out and start a long-planned sewing project.

I'm making a retro 1950s apron to wear when I'm baking. I'm using a pretty Parisian scene print in shades of pink and blue and trimming it with a pink and white gingham fabric and blue ric-rac. Cutting out the fabric takes much longer than anticipated and I've barely started sewing when Mr Candytuft arrives home. I put my sewing aside when he announces that we need to go out and buy supplies for the garden.

We are still getting to know the shops in our area and are unsure of what is available or where to look. We try what we think is a farm supplies shop, only to discover it is a feed store. We then head to a building supplies store and they direct us to their garden centre, where we finally find what we are looking for: we buy metal posts to support garden netting for my sweet peas to climb. I started these from seed and they are still in pots when they should have been planted weeks ago.

When we get home, this job is put on hold whilst we concentrate on planting the front garden bed with the perennials we bought more than a month ago at the garden club's plant sale. Since we have already done all the hard work clearing the bed of grass and weeds, we want to get everything planted before the weeds return and before the bad weather, which is forecast to arrive later this evening. We work together and get the plants in the ground in less than two hours.

I salvage a few of my annual seedlings and add them to the bed: most of my seedlings died due to the unseasonal weather during what was supposedly spring.

Sunday is a dull and dismal morning with low cloud and the promise of yet more rain to come. In an effort to bring some summer cheer to what is actually Midsummer's Day, I bake another lemon drizzle cake. We enjoy it fresh and still warm from the oven – a citrusy zing of Mediterranean flavour being the only hint of summer around here. The forecast for the next twenty-four hours is still worse, with torrential rain and cold temperatures continuing.

I read a report on CBC News about Christmas trees being yet another casualty of the heavy frosts of early June. It may seem odd to be talking of Christmas trees at this time of year, but these are growing on a Christmas tree farm in Kilmuir, Prince Edward Island. The frosts damaged the new growth on the tips of the trees, causing them to develop dead, brown buds. The long-term effect of this is that half of this year's crop will not be fit for sale this Christmas.

***

An unexpected break in the weather arrives a few days later and it feels like summer might actually have arrived. As it is so warm indoors, neither of us feels like cooking and we don't have anything suitable for the barbecue, so we decide to have dinner at the local hotel, where we enjoy steak and chips, which is their 'two for one' special for June. Going out for dinner is a rare treat and the hotel is close enough that we can walk home in minutes.

The following morning, Mr Candytuft decides we are going out for breakfast at a local bakery. It is a beautiful morning and already warming up to be a hot day. After breakfast, he decides to take me for a drive to show me the places that he has visited on his bike rides. We go down to Linkletter Provincial Park, which is also a campsite and busy with summer visitors. Located on the shore, there is a beach and a sea view. Afterwards, we head down to the boardwalk for some exercise. I am surprised by how lush the vegetation looks after only a few warm days and by the number of wild flowers now in bloom. Along the highway, we see lupins coming into flower, which is a definite sign that summer is here.

We are now at the end of the last week of June. Friday morning starts off wet and cool but, by lunchtime, there is a dramatic change as the heat arrives and with it, the humidity. By mid-afternoon, it is 25°C but it feels like 30°C with the humidity. The air has that muggy, stale feeling, like stepping out of the shower in a steamy bathroom.

We visit the garden centre to buy tomato plants to replace those I grew from seed, but lost to the poor weather conditions this spring, and return with four plants of a vine tomato variety called 'Sweetheart of the Patio'. Our purchases include garden mulch to suppress weeds in the front garden. I plan to be environmentally friendly and lay newspaper before covering with mulch. I've read that matting used under mulch contains plastic and also prevents insects and worms from coming up from the ground. As we seem to have a lot of worms, we are concerned for their welfare, as they look after the soil.

The tomatoes are planted in our VegTrug and watered in well. Two seedlings of the variety 'Matt's Wild Cherry' have survived, so we leave them in the hope that their growth will pick up, now the hot weather has arrived.

This evening, we are on a severe thunderstorm watch after this first hot day of summer. The sky, which was almost cloudless earlier in the day, starts to change to a greyish-blue base layer, which darkens at a higher altitude. I watch as a massive cloud develops to the west – it balloons and quickly gains height: vertical accumulation is the first warning of a thunder-cloud formation. To the east, the sky is still virtually cloudless with a haze of pink streaked with blue on the horizon. The heat has also brought out the mosquitoes, which swarm by our windows searching for admittance: thank goodness for window screens!

The cloud continues to build as the thunder-clouds roll in; the darkest of which is centred to the west, where the sky is now black. Huge banks of dark grey clouds roll overhead. I hear distant rumbling and it seems that life has stood still outdoors, aside from the mosquitoes. There is a flash of lightning and I go around the house closing windows before the anticipated downpour. The wind blows through the pine trees in our garden and their tops wave and bend as the storm gathers strength. The heavy rain arrives, but the sky quickly changes colour to reddish-grey on the horizon as the sun sets: the downpour is short-lived.

The eerie silence continues; the only audible noise now is the wind and the ticking of the mantelpiece clock. I look out and the street is deserted, as everyone has settled in for the long weekend. The severe thunderstorm watch has ended and we can sleep soundly tonight.

***

It is Canada Day weekend and time for a nationwide party. Canada Day celebrates the anniversary of 1 July 1867 when the four separate colonies of Ontario, Quebec, Nova Scotia and New Brunswick united into a single Dominion within the British Empire, called Canada. This day was originally known as Dominion Day but was renamed in 1982.

Our long weekend starts with breakfast at the local bakery. On our way to the restaurant, we pass lupins lining the sides of the highway. Unlike earlier in the week, when they were barely starting to open, they are now in full bloom, in shades of pink and purple. Their spires of flowers punctuate the surrounding vegetation with bright colours. They are a positive sign that summer on the Island has officially started.

After breakfast, Mr Candytuft decides to go for a ride on his bike and I head into town in search of plants for the garden. At the garden centre, I buy lavender for a hedge at the front of our newly created flower bed; borage to encourage the bees to our garden and alpine strawberries to grow in our VegTrug. The lady at the garden centre reminds me that they have an event taking place this morning, as there is a falconry presentation. I drop by to talk to the handler and to admire the hawks. There is a Harris hawk, which is a medium-sized male. His bold markings are dark brown and chestnut red, with a white-tipped tail. He has long yellow legs and yellow markings on his face, with a yellow, hook-shaped beak. His handler is wearing a leather gauntlet and the hawk is perched on his hand.

The second bird is a kestrel with magnificent plumage in cream and conker brown. Its breast is speckled and its wings are brown. It is hooded to keep it calm, so I am able to stand close to it and admire this beautiful bird without it being aware of my presence.

On my way home, I stop at the Dollar Store to buy some Maple Leaf flags for Canada Day tomorrow. I find a headband with two flags attached to miniature flag poles and buy it. I visit the supermarket to buy supplies for a picnic, which I am planning for tomorrow. The shop is packed with customers stocking up for the long weekend.

I arrive home with a car laden with stuff. Between us, we unload, before Mr Candytuft announces we should go back out and buy more strawberry plants – we return to town, only to discover they are sold out.

The day is blazing hot and the sun is high in the sky. I feel dehydrated after being out for most of the day, despite drinking a bottle of water on the way home. As a last-ditch attempt, we visit a nursery out of town and our efforts are rewarded. We find ever-bearing strawberries and buy four plants. I discover that they have large hollyhocks and we add one to the cart, as all those I have already planted are too small to flower this year (and last year's plants didn't survive the winter).

We finally arrive home and it is already mid-afternoon. After a late lunch, I change and go out into the garden to do some planting. It is a hot and sultry afternoon when most people are relaxing and enjoying a beer (I saw some of them outside the hotel near where we live), rather than working in the heat.

I'm on the back deck when I hear a loud buzzing. I investigate the source, looking through a stack of empty plant pots and discover a trapped bumblebee. I release it and it takes flight, pausing as if in thanks for its rescue, before flying off into the garden.

I plant alpine strawberries, lavender and borage, in addition to filling three containers with petunias in two shades of pink and purple, which I bought at the garden centre for the bargain price of 99 cents each. Two green containers are placed on either side of the front door, the bright colours of the flowers contrasting well with their pots. The third container is placed close to the back door.

Mr Candytuft kindly offers to go out and water for me after the latest World Cup match has finished. He returns, complaining of big mosquito bites. I have managed to avoid being bitten today, but I did take the precaution of covering myself in bug repellent before venturing outdoors. I'm leaving a trail of citronella in my wake, but it seems to be working.

The final addition to the front garden is the planting of our three Maple Leaf flags in the flower bed. They bravely flutter in the wind. We are now officially ready for Canada Day.

CHAPTER ELEVEN

JULY: SUMMER GARDENS

C anada Day begins overcast but quickly clears when the sun appears in an almost cloudless sky. Mr Candytuft decides to head out for a bike ride and I go for a morning walk before the heat of the day. I'm not back long when Mr Candytuft arrives home.

I spend time in the kitchen preparing food for a picnic. I had wanted to have a picnic to mark Midsummer's Day last weekend, but the day was rainy, so I postponed my plan until today.

We get ready and go out to join the celebrations in the Acadian community of Wellington, arriving as the live entertainment is starting. We are in a park and the setting is adjacent to the river with a footbridge giving access to the opposite bank. Searching for somewhere to sit, we and cross the bridge to a bench where we can enjoy our picnic but still hear the music.

We tuck into finger sandwiches of smoked salmon and cream cheese; cream cheese and cucumber and mini quiches and hors d'oeuvres. These are followed by freshly baked scones. The picnic is delicious, but the mosquitoes are bothersome, even though I took the precaution of covering exposed skin in citronella repellent.

Moving to the main seating area, we seek shade in a place where we can listen to the live performances. I have my Canadian Maple Leaf flag headband with me, but remove it in favour of a hat, to shade me from the sun. The audience is seated in front of the stage and their clothing is a sea of red and white. 'I am Canadian' shirts abound and one lady in the crowd is wearing a tee shirt with the logo, 'Kiss me, I'm Canadian'!

I spot a woman moving through the crowd and point her out to Mr Candytuft. She is wearing a beige hat with a beaver on top of it, bedecked with the Canadian Maple Leaf flag. As she approaches, Mr Candytuft tells her that I like her hat and asks if we can take a photo. She comes over and greets me and suggests we have our photo taken together. She is French-Canadian and asks where we are from. She tells us she was born just down the road and has lived here all of her life. She says that there are strong cultural roots in the village, which is a thriving community and that the performers are all locals.

The music is a mix of styles – ballads initially – and the commentary switches seamlessly between French and English. After the ballads, there is some traditional Acadian music, which soon has feet tapping along. There are a couple of girls who come onto the stage to perform some step dancing, followed by a mother and daughter. Step dancing has a long history in both Acadian and Celtic communities across Prince Edward Island. The dancing is fast-paced, with intricate footwork and is accompanied by traditional fiddle music.

The second set of the afternoon is performed by a family group and they play a variety of different styles of music. They are joined on stage by an accordion player and there is a rapid increase in the pace of the music.

The finale is a performance of 'O Canada', performed on a saw – yes, the father of the family takes a saw and bends it, then plays it with a bow. This gets the loudest cheers and applause of the day.

We move off and return to the car. Mr Candytuft takes me to

see a beautiful garden, which he has spotted when he has been out on his bike, and then we turn towards home. On our way back, we pull over to the side of the road to photograph the lupins, which look absolutely stunning in the summer sunshine. It has been a memorable day and we are glad we made the effort to get out and explore, as well as participating in Canada's national holiday.

The following morning, we are out for a walk on the boardwalk before the heat arrives. It is Monday of the long weekend and there are quite a lot of walkers and cyclists out enjoying an extra day off. Afterwards, we work in the garden. I'm adding cedar mulch to our newly created flower bed in the front garden: I chose red mulch, which matches the colour of the red earth.

Mr Candytuft is working in our vegetable patch – erecting posts to support netting for French beans. Both jobs take longer than anticipated, during which time the sun breaks through the clouds, the temperature and humidity start to climb and the mosquitoes come out in force. We are both relieved to get back indoors and have acquired more bites, which seem to be trophies of any attempt to spend time outdoors.

Environment Canada has issued a heat warning for the Maritimes, and Prince Edward Island experiences a week of high temperatures and high humidity. The scorching temperatures and humid conditions leave us feeling exhausted.

**

After three months of working in the convenience store, an opportunity presents itself to leave the world of retail and move to a job in a medical clinic, which is more suited to my previous experience. I feel a certain sense of relief because I've survived the world of retail and also an admiration for my co-workers, who are all hard-working and cheerful, even when getting up for work well before dawn. I will miss working with them.

My first few days in my new job see me on orientation and I enjoy the familiarity of a clinic environment and having time to chat to the patients. I feel much more at home than in my previous job and I'm relieved to be able to sit down at work, rather than being on my feet and standing for the entire shift.

***

An appointment in Charlottetown during the first week of July sees us travelling on a Friday morning. The forecast is for thunderstorms later in the day, but the sky is already ominous. We do some shopping in town to stock up on a few groceries, then head home.

The drive home is a wet one. The rain pounds down and squalls significantly reduce visibility. It eases off a bit, only to get heavy again further along the highway. We arrive home and I run for cover. Mr Candytuft unloads the car whilst I make tea and put the groceries away. The weather front and resulting storms bring the humidity down. The ominous sky before sunset is a picture of dark grey rolling clouds in front of a backdrop of lighter grey and white wispy streaks with the sun shining low on the horizon. The overnight temperature falls to 11°C.

Saturday morning dawns bright with a brisk breeze and a sunny, blue sky, with barely a cloud visible. Mr Candytuft plans to watch the World Cup quarter-finals, so I head out alone for a bit of culture. Before I leave, I peg laundry out on the line – five pegs secure each of the sheets, which are soon flapping like sails. I've learned that it is essential to use lots of pegs on days like this, if I am not to return home to find the laundry on the ground.

I am heading to Bedeque, a village about twenty minutes' drive from home, for the opening of a new exhibition at the Bedeque Area Historical Museum. This year's exhibits are related to the settlement of the United Empire Loyalist families around Bedeque Bay, in 1784.

The US War of Independence saw the families who were

loyal to the British Crown relocate to Canada. Amongst those who arrived was William Schurman, who settled on an area known as Lot 26, in 1784. The area where he chose to settle is on the south side of the Dunk River: the land is at the head of the estuary, in the area now known as Central Bedeque. At the time, Prince Edward Island was known as St John's Island and the 1798 Census recorded that William's son Peter was also living on Lot 26. In 1808, William used profits from his farm and shipbuilding yard to buy 6,500 acres of land, for which he paid £800.

Part of the exhibition tells the story of the Valley Farm, which has been in the Schurman family since 1839. It is a fascinating glimpse at the history of this part of Prince Edward Island and there is a wealth of documents and photographs going back through eight generations of the Schurman family, descendants of which formally open this year's exhibition.

The weather is glorious and the fresh breeze is a welcome respite from the humidity, which is forecast to return next week. In the afternoon, we start planting our vegetable garden. It is the end of the first week of July and we are only starting our garden.

Mr Candytuft has spent the last couple of days getting it prepared and stringing nets to support our crops. We sow three varieties of French beans, three of peas and two varieties of lettuce, all of which are being grown from seed. The sweet peas, which I grew from seed during our absent spring, are planted at the end of the vegetable garden, to take advantage of the support structure and netting. Any further planting is put on hold due to another quarter-final match for the World Cup. Mr Candytuft does not want to miss it and I can't do any further planting at present because he wants to do some more digging first.

This Sunday marks the start of the Summerside Garden Club's garden tours, which will continue over six weekends. These open gardens are an opportunity to go out and see what other gardeners are growing and to admire their hard work.

Our first visit takes us to a pretty garden filled with beautiful flowers: a pale pink peony attracts my attention, as it is absolutely covered in flowers. I bury my nose in it and enjoy its fresh floral scent. We chat to the owner of the garden and ask her when she planted her vegetable garden, which is looking extremely bountiful, with peas and beans, as well as tomatoes, all growing well. There is an extensive strawberry patch and a second patch of rhubarb. The flowers include hollyhocks, which are already in bud – I would have liked to see them flowering, but it is a bit too early for them. Our host offers refreshments and I enjoy a glass of tangy homemade lemonade – perfect for a hot afternoon.

We move on to the second open garden, which is filled with roses in shades of red, pink and white. They tumble over the garden fence, but I am a little disappointed that most of them are not perfumed, being of the opinion that there is little point in growing a rose that does not have a beautiful fragrance. One of the roses is a deep pink with large open blooms and this one has a gorgeous scent, which is some compensation for the lack of scent in its companions.

In the back garden, we discover more peonies in pale pink and cream. Their huge flowers are filled with scent, which wafts across the garden on the breeze: this inspires me to want to grow some of my own. Blue campanula flowers also catch my eye: their bell-shaped blooms are so delicate and pretty.

The third garden is very different because it is a woodcarver's garden. We have driven past on numerous occasions and the sight of the carved totem topped by a bald eagle is one that I remember from our arrival last summer. This garden is definitely drawing the largest crowds and there are people milling around the garden. We approach a peaceful space called 'The Healing Garden', where wind chimes are softly playing in the breeze and my eye is caught by the carvings in every direction. There is a full-size carving that resembles Gandalf from *The Lord of the Rings*, a fisherman with his net and a bear amongst the trees, but the one that draws my attention is that of a majestic bald eagle sitting on a tree stump. The carvings are tactile and I run my hand over them, wondering how anyone can create such beautiful works of art with a chainsaw.

There are a couple of water features with the softly bubbling sound of the water adding to the sense of well-being and tranquillity. The trees provide much-needed shade, which encourages visitors to linger and enjoy the garden. One feature that captures my imagination is a fairy garden. The fairies appear to be dancing amongst the flowers – tiny white alyssum is the perfect height for a fairy to hide, as are a couple of ceramic toadstools.

We have enjoyed the garden tours and stop off at a local garden centre on our way home, where I buy some peonies for our garden. We probably won't get flowers this year, as it is late to be planting them, but imagine how beautiful it will look next year when 'Sarah Bernhardt' (with pastel-pink double flowers), 'Duchesse de Nemours' (ivory white flowers with the scent of Lily of the Valley) and 'Alexander Fleming' (with large deep rose-pink flowers) put on a show next spring.

***

It is the weekend of the Lobster Carnival, an annual event in Summerside since its inception in 1956. The origins of this event stem from the original organising committee's expectation that it would 'focus attention on the town and would bring in a larger number of summer visitors'. As the carnival reached sixty years in 2016, it could be described as a shining success and one of the highlights of the summer season.

The three-day event is a mixture of entertainment with live performances by local musicians, a circus and midway or fair, with all the thrills and excitement of the rides and amusements, at the carnival grounds, as well as lobster preparation demonstrations and tastings. Other events at the Summerside Raceway include harness racing and seafood evenings.

Saturday's events start with a Lobster Carnival Parade through the town – the crowds are out in force to watch, as seventy floats crawl along the route. It is another hot day, so many choose to shelter beneath the shade of big trees lining the route, as generations of families share the tradition of attending this event. Floats include a contingent from the crew of *HMCS Summerside*, the bagpipes and drums of the College of Piping, police outriders and an enormous model of a red lobster on a bed of straw, which is the carnival's mascot.

The highlight of the day, for us, is the boat race. Mention a boat race to anyone who grew up in the UK and most people would immediately think of The Boat Race, which is an annual rowing race between the Oxford University Boat Club and the Cambridge University Boat Club, which takes place on the River Thames.

The boat race at the Summerside Lobster Carnival is in a league of its own because it is a cardboard boat race and far more fun. We join the crowds assembling at the pond at Spinnaker's Landing and anticipation mounts as the start time approaches. There are spectators surrounding the pond, some brave souls sitting on the rocks in full sun, whilst others, including ourselves, have chosen the shade of the pastel-coloured gift and souvenir shops, in shades of yellow, pink and green.

We see a couple of boats drawn up close to the shore on the far side of the pond and people milling about in preparation for the event. Finally, life jackets are donned and the fun begins. The teams compete in heats of two at a time. The first to compete are a team of four in a yellow boat against a team of two from the local dairy in a grey boat. The crowd goes wild, cheering on the competitors. The actual course is a bit vague, but the general idea seems to be to paddle across the pond, before turning and paddling back. The first boats stand up to the challenge and their crews make it safely back to shore.

The crews in the second heat are not so lucky. There are two grey boats in this heat, the second of which makes it across the pond, but capsizes on the way back, much to the delight of the crowd. The two crew members swim back to the shore with their craft accompanied by loud cheers and applause.

The third heat involves a boat called *Banana Splash*, which is painted yellow and looks completely unstable (it is shaped like a banana). It has a crew of three children, and there is an adult in the stern, who seems to be acting as ballast. They compete against a grey shark boat (complete with a fearsome set of teeth at the bow), with a crew of two. It is a close-run heat but *Banana Splash* is first to finish. The next heat is far more competitive as it is the Navy against the College of Piping, who have brought their own piper to the event. The College of Piping won this event in 2017, whilst the crew of *HMCS Summerside* are hoping to redeem themselves after being the first boat to sink.

The Navy's boat is a two-man frigate complete with a cardboard gun on the bow and the Navy Ensign on the stern. The College of Piping's boat is decorated in the style of a Viking long-boat. The team receives a stirring send-off as they are piped into the water.

The Navy win this heat and go on to compete in the final against *Banana Splash*. There is a battle to the finish, with both teams splashing each other, creating waves that capsize *Banana Splash*, much to the amusement and delight of the crowd. We all give both teams a big cheer and lots of applause as the Navy wins this year's competition.

It has been a hugely entertaining afternoon and we have thoroughly enjoyed this event, but we are glad to head home to get some relief from the heat and humidity. We both feel fried from the intensity of the sun and are more than happy to have cooling showers and spend the rest of the day in the shade.

Sunday afternoon arrives and we are on our way to the second open garden event of the Summerside Garden Club. We drive out to the neighbouring town of Kensington, where we visit a delightful garden and chat with the lady who is responsible for its development and upkeep. At about half an acre, it is a sizeable plot and it contains a magnificent horse chestnut tree, which provides much-needed shade on this hot afternoon. On closer inspection, we see there are tiny conkers developing, which are already spiky, but bright green in their immature state. A garden obelisk supports two roses in shades of pink. On the other side of the lawn, there is a sweet little cream shed with white shutters on the windows and a purple clematis climbing up a trellis.

Beyond the shed lies the vegetable garden, which already promises a bountiful harvest. It is filled with tomatoes, peas, leeks, cucumbers, peppers and a variety of herbs. We chat about planting and learn that most of the vegetables were grown from plants, rather than seeds, and they have only been in the ground about a month.

We drive back into town to visit the second garden on our list. This town garden is a much smaller plot but is filled with an array of mature shrubs and perennials, as well as window boxes of colourful red geraniums. Tall spires of blue delphiniums punctuate the back of a mixed border of perennial geraniums, red *achillea* and yellow *Alchemilla mollis*.

We journey out of town and into the countryside for the final garden of the day. Properties are identified by civic address numbers, which are not always prominently displayed. We miss the house we are searching for and have to retrace our steps.

The garden awaiting us is magical and by far the most beautiful garden we have visited. It has shade trees beneath one of which is a white bicycle, propped against the trunk and adorned with bunting. Large shrubs keep things hidden, necessitating an exploration. We find a model of a white sheep with a crown peeping out from amongst the foliage. There are wooden stars and signs beneath the window boxes of red geraniums, one of which says 'Homestead'. A pergola with hanging baskets of red and white geraniums is at the front door.

Passing around the side of the house, we discover an adorable baby barn decorated with a willow wreath and candle lights in the windows, which is surrounded by red flowers cascading around and in front of it. We are welcomed by the owners, who invite us to enjoy their garden.

We wander across the lawn, where tree stumps have been left as a habitat for wildlife. There is a huge barn with a grey tin roof, which is adorned with nesting boxes, and there are quirky little touches to the garden, which surprise and delight us, such as the iron bedstead we discover in a shady spot. It is made up with pristine white linen and a nightdress is laid across it. A teddy bear is propped against the pillow and the whole scene invites us to take a nap in the shade – but we resist! There is a luggage label at the foot of the bed, which reads, 'I'm going to make everything around me beautiful – that will be my life.' What a beautiful sentiment.

I step onto the deck at the rear of the house to discover the source of running water – there is a fountain in the shade. Close by, a model of the Tin Man from *The Wizard of Oz* hangs from a tree branch.

Further, around the deck, I find a fireplace with a mantelpiece and mirror. It is white, with plants growing from the hearth. A couple of chairs nearby invite the owners to pause for a while and enjoy this shady spot.

We chat with the owners before we leave. They started this garden from scratch fifteen years ago and we all agree that to be a gardener, patience is essential. When they first arrived, there was one small flower bed at the front of the house. Now, it is a peaceful retreat and filled with birds, including hummingbirds, which are frequent summer visitors.

We leave the garden filled with inspiration for what can be achieved in a garden over time. Ours won't look like this any time soon, but we can dream…

The following afternoon finds us working in our vegetable garden. It is already hot and humid and it isn't long before I seek shelter in the shade. We are still sowing seeds and add two rows of beetroot and a row of carrots. The French beans, which were sown less than ten days ago, have germinated, and are putting on a growth spurt. Mr Candytuft is convinced they have grown since this morning.

I add a couple of rows of cosmos seeds – all of my seedlings died in the cold, wet weather of what passed for spring. I'm hopeful they will grow fast and I can still add some late colour to our front garden, as well as enjoy them as cut flowers. Once these are all sown, along with a few dill seeds, I return to the shade indoors and a cooling shower. I intend to spend the rest of the afternoon close to the fan and drink lots of fluids.

A couple of days later, I go for a walk along the boardwalk. The weather has been so hot that I haven't been down here for a while and Mr Candytuft has decided he would prefer to go for a bike ride. The day is hot and humid, with high temperatures forecast for this afternoon.

The heat of the past few days has brought the wild roses into bloom, in various shades of pink, with yellow anthers; they are a magnet for the bees and other insects. On my return trip, I pick one flower to take home.

I've wanted to try watercolour painting for ages and recently invested in a set of paints – a palette called Decadent Pies – which I chose because they reflect the colours of Prince Edward Island. I have brushes and paper and set to work on my painting once I return home. I am hesitant at first, but soon start outlining my rose. I don't have a pink in my palette and seem unable to mix these paints, so I settle on a shade called guava meringue, which produces a pretty apricot rose. I find the whole process surprisingly satisfying and I'm pleased I have plucked up the courage to try painting, as I was useless at art at school. I show my painting to Mr Candytuft, who expresses surprise when I tell him that I painted it – he thought it was a photocopy!

On Sunday morning, I go for a walk around our neighbourhood, whilst Mr Candytuft opts to go for a bike ride. When I get home, I spend some time pottering in the garden. I pick tomatoes, which are starting to ripen. I deadhead my petunias and water them with my watering can. They are looking good in spite of the heat and are covered in flowers, in shades of pink and purple. Their green foliage contrasts well with the green of their containers. It is already too hot for any strenuous activity, so I head indoors out of the sun.

The afternoon turns out to be another scorcher and the humidity is high. We are on our way to the beach and drive to Cabot Beach Provincial Park, which is the largest park in western Prince Edward Island. It is located on Malpeque Bay and is a popular spot, both with campers and day visitors.

We park in the area for day visitors and walk across the park to the beach, descending onto a flat, sandy beach that is busy with families enjoying a Sunday out. We pass through the supervised beach area, where there are lifeguards on duty, and head for the shore. The tide is on its way in, but there are still a couple of hours until high tide.

We paddle in the shallows – the water is about 17°C – not bad, considering that this is the north shore of the Island and these are the waters of the Gulf of Saint Lawrence. We last visited this beach shortly after we arrived on Prince Edward Island and it is surprising how much it has changed. At the time, there was a relatively short stretch of beach to walk on and a sort of tidal lagoon, which we could not cross. Now, that whole area is a sandy beach and to the western end, there is a shallow pool of water that has been warmed by the sun and is a magnet for families – children are able to paddle without getting out of their depth.

There is something very calming about walking barefoot on the sand and feeling at one with nature. I wade through the water and enjoy its cooling effect on this hot afternoon. I am wearing a wide-brimmed straw hat to protect me from the sun, as I burn easily, as well as sunscreen. After a while, I've had enough of being in full sun and walk back to the car to await Mr Candytuft's return, as he has chosen to paddle for a while longer.

As I come off the beach, I stop at a convenient tap with a length of hose attached, and rinse the sand from my feet. The water is cold and refreshing. I would almost be tempted to rinse my face and hair if the hose were a little longer.

Mr Candytuft returns shortly after – I've drunk a large bottle of water whilst I have been waiting, but still feel dehydrated. We arrive home and I enjoy a cooling shower and then seek relief from the heat in front of the fan. On days like these, it is fun to go for a walk on the beach, but I am only too glad to return home.

The next morning, I'm in the kitchen and making healthy snacks. I make Bakewell tart balls with dates, sultana, cranberries and cashews, and raw chocolate truffle balls. It is too hot for baking, but these only require a blitz in the food processor and time in the fridge to set. These have become firm favourites in our diet since I first made them some weeks ago.

The hot, sultry days of July are making me lazy. It feels like too much effort going out for a walk, but I decide to take a shorter stroll along the boardwalk. It is late morning and the sun is high in the sky and the temperature is already at 30°C. This afternoon, the humidex (combined temperature and humidity value), is expected to reach 36°C.

I walk along the shore: there is an onshore breeze, which offers some relief from the oppressive heat. The sea looks conker-brown in the shallower waters of the harbour, as the red sandy bottom is being churned up: the water offshore looks a deep shade of green. Whitecaps are dancing across the waves like wild horses.

I pause at the stream, but the muskrats have left. Both streams where we watched them swimming and playing earlier in the year have become overgrown and murky due to lack of water flow. Mr Candytuft talked to a conservation officer a few weeks ago, when a team were working in the stream, and attempting to increase the flow. They placed logs in both streams to narrow them, but it seems their attempts have been in vain, as the water is stagnant and the muskrats have moved on. It is such a shame they have disappeared because they were a magnet for visitors of all ages, who paused to observe them in their natural habitat.

A twenty-minute walk gets some sea air into my lungs and I enjoy the change of scene, but I'm relieved to be back at the car and on my way. My normal walk covers three times this distance and takes a little under an hour, but I couldn't face it in this heat.

Back at home, I hang the laundry out to dry. It is a windy afternoon and it dries quickly, but I'm in no rush to stand out in the sun, taking it off the line. I prefer the relative cool of being indoors and out of the sun. It feels like the dog days of summer have arrived and it is time to slow down.

It is the last weekend of July and we plan to attend the open gardens this afternoon, but the day starts off overcast and it is not long before the rain is pounding down. The clouds roll across the sky and the sun comes out, then, at the time when the gardens are due to open, we get another cloudburst. As neither of us wishes to be soaked to the skin, we sit at home and are resigned to not going out, but then the sun pops out from behind the clouds and the skies clear.

We drive into town and visit the first garden on our list. A walk around the back of a bungalow leads to the discovery of a garden that is absolutely filled with colour. Daylilies in shades of orange, yellow and pink are dotted throughout the garden and the plot is deceptive in its size. It extends to the border of arable land in which potatoes, for which Prince Edward Island is famous, are already in flower. The flowers of the borders merge with the flowers of the potatoes, so the garden appears to go on forever.

We met the owner of this garden at the garden club's perennial plant sale in late May: he welcomes us to his garden and offers refreshment on this hot afternoon. Ice-cold water is in a cooler in the shade and we are only too happy to accept a bottle each. After browsing around the garden, we seek shelter in the shade of a tree and chat with other visitors.

We move on to the second garden where we discover an

enormous garden behind an average-sized residential house. This garden is absolutely stunning and is owned by the past president of the garden club. She welcomes us to her garden and invites us to look around. There is a potting shed tucked away to one side and a stunning pond with a fountain of a Greek maiden bearing a ewer on her shoulder. Goldfish swim in the shallows, concealed under rocks. The pond is sited amongst the trees and is surrounded by flowers.

Winding paths lead us through flower beds packed with perennials and mature shrubs, then on to a gazebo and a thyme walk, the fragrance of which wafts over us as we meander through the garden. A huge blue spruce is sited at the end of the garden, along with other mature trees.

Turning our steps back towards the house, we stop to chat with the owners. This is a garden that has developed over a considerable time – they moved to their home in 1972.

The next garden is a short distance out of town. It is another surprise in terms of size, as it extends over what must be several acres and faces onto the river. We walk around and admire the planting, but cut this visit short because the mosquitoes are out and I'm getting badly bitten. We have come out today with two different treatments for bites, but I don't wish to hang around long enough to add any further bites to my collection.

Having retraced our steps back to town, we visit the last garden on the list. We are welcomed by the owner, who tells us that there are actually two gardens to visit. Both she and her neighbour are members of the garden club and have opened both gardens to visitors.

Located in a quiet residential street, these gardens are more modest plots, but they are absolutely packed with flowers. There are window boxes and gazebos – one over a vegetable garden, which has been imaginatively planted to blend in with the rest of the garden, whilst the one next door supports a grapevine. We are offered a seat in the shade and chilled fruit punch for refreshment. The owner tells us she is also a new member of the garden club, but she has tended this plot for the past forty years, so it is no surprise that it looks so perfect.

My attention is caught by the little finishing touches in both gardens – a bicycle propped up against a tree, which is supporting baskets of flowers. Window boxes overflowing with trailing plants and pink and purple petunias. A fountain in the corner of the garden, which is a child looking into a pond. The sound of gently running water is soothing to the senses. The doorways of both homes are surrounded by flowering plants and there is a sweet little model of a dog sitting on the doorstep of one home, waiting to greet visitors.

We take home lots of ideas and inspiration but think that we will have to wait a few weeks before we can do any further improvements to our garden. The general opinion of other garden club members is that September will be a nice month and it should be cool enough by then for larger garden projects.

I'm in the kitchen after we return home and busy slicing lemons, oranges, cucumber and strawberries, to which I add mint and lots of ice and lemonade. I'm making Pimm's – the quintessential drink of the long, hot days of summer (made from herb-infused gin). I recall the first time that I made this some years ago. I offered Mr Candytuft a glass after he had been working in the garden. He drank a glass in seconds before asking for a refill. I think he was on his third glass before he asked what was in it – he thought it was lemonade – since that time, I've referred to it as lemonade with flavouring. It is a most refreshing drink on a summer's afternoon and one glass is never enough.

CHAPTER TWELVE

AUGUST: HISTORY AND HERITAGE

I have wanted to learn more about the history and heritage of the Acadians on Prince Edward Island since visiting the Acadian community of Wellington for their Canada Day celebrations. We decide to visit the Acadian Museum in the village of Miscouche, where we are made welcome. Our visit starts with a short film about the history of the Acadians, before browsing through their exhibits.

The Acadians are descendants of French colonists who came to North America from 1604 onwards: most of them originated from western France. They settled and formed a community known as Acadie, in what is now mainland Nova Scotia.

The territory that formed the land on which they settled was of strategic importance to both the English and the French and it changed hands seven times before the signing of the Treaty of Utrecht in 1713 when France was forced to hand over Acadie to Great Britain.

The Acadians were deported from their land and scattered amongst the British colonies along the Atlantic seaboard. A small number of Acadian families moved to Île Saint-Jean (present-day Prince Edward Island), which was under French control. France established her first colony on the island in the summer of 1720, when about two hundred settlers came over and the Acadians joined the French settlers. The Acadians were farmers and cultivated land along the rivers and bays where there were natural meadows. Their main crops were wheat and peas – the main ingredients for bread and soup – their staple diet. The community grew in number as about 1,500 Acadians moved to Île Saint-Jean when the British began deportations from the mainland in 1755.

Those Acadians who didn't escape deportation were forced onto ships bound for France, two of which sank in storms, and many Acadian families died on the journey when sickness spread through the passengers. Of those who survived, some families returned to the island between 1758 and 1860, where they were forced to rent their land from English landlords. This caused considerable hardship to many families, forcing them to start clearing their own land and obtaining proper title, which allowed them to establish their own schools and communities. They lived separately from the English-speaking Islanders and there was no integration, as they struggled to survive in a subsistence economy.

From 1860 onwards, the Acadian community made efforts to achieve the same socio-economic status enjoyed by other Islanders, whilst maintaining their own identity and heritage. They adopted the Acadian flag in 1884 – the French Tricolour of three vertical bands in blue, white and red, with a yellow star, which represents the star of Mary, Stella Maris, Patron Saint of the Acadians. At the same time, they adopted the Latin hymn, 'Ave Maris Stella', which translates as 'Hail, Star of the Sea', as the Acadian national anthem.

It took until the year 2000 and a battle all the way to the Supreme Court of Canada, for Acadian parents and organisations to win the right for Francophones in minority situations to have access to French-language schools in their communities. Today, there are six French-language schools located throughout Prince Edward Island and people of Acadian descent account for twenty-five per cent of the Island population.

Prince Edward Island is a bilingual province: English and French are the two official languages of Canada. Both languages are used on road signs, maps, tourist brochures and packaging of all goods sold in Canada.

Although English is the predominant language of Prince Edward Island, French is spoken widely, especially in Acadian and Francophone communities. Over 5,000 people (2006 figures) speak French as their first language. Concentrations of Acadians are found to the west of the province in the Evangeline area, as well as in the Island's second city, Summerside, where there is a French-language school, aptly named, École-sur-Mer. This was initially opened as an elementary school before expanding to include junior high school grades. In November of 2017, it was announced by the provincial government of Prince Edward Island, that they had committed $5 million to bring high school facilities to the Summerside French School.

Of course, it is important to remember that there are a people whose history predates the British and the French. Prince Edward Island has been inhabited for at least 10,000 years: these Aboriginal people are the Mi'kmaq, who called the island, Abegweit, which means 'Cradled on the Waves'.

The Mi'kmaq lived along the rivers and coast and depended on hunting and fishing. Their descendants live on the Island to this day and the Abegweit is one of two Prince Edward Island First Nations, the other being the Territory of Lennox Island in western Prince Edward Island. Abegweit is a First Nation band or government, which governs three reserves that are separated geographically but are administered jointly, and are served by a Chief and two Councillors. The First Nation provides services to the community as well as settling any disputes.

Like their Acadian neighbours, the Abegweit Mi'kmaw Nation want to participate in the modern economy of their land, but also honour their culture, language and traditions. They promote the importance of education, provide training opportunities for young entrepreneurs and own and operate a variety of businesses on the Island.

***

The heat and humidity of July continue into August. Our raised vegetable garden is flourishing and I start harvesting what promises to be a large crop of tomatoes, which are ripening fast. The dog days of summer have definitely arrived and we are wilting fast in the heat. Everything takes a supreme amount of effort in these conditions, so I'm only too happy to put my feet up in the afternoon if I'm not actually at work. I have a couple of weeks off and intend to enjoy the summer.

We meet our new neighbours, who move in at the beginning of the month: weeks of frenzied construction work took place next door as contractors finished the renovations of their new home.

Our maritime weather results in torrential downpours, as summer storms roll in, one of which results in monsoon-like conditions, with hailstones and driving rain and winds. Everyone dives for cover and people who were in a hurry to go about their business suddenly have time to wait out the storms indoors, rather than make a dash for their cars. Some storms last for the entire day and continue into the night. We have a couple of weekends where the best place to be is indoors.

Two whole weeks of extreme heat and humidity cause heat alerts to be issued by Environment Canada on a daily basis and the humidex reaches 41°C. We try to arrange our days so that any physical activity, such as walking or going for a bike ride (Mr Candytuft's favourite form of exercise these days) take place early in the day, when the temperatures are a little cooler, though no less humid. Sleeping at night is almost impossible because of the build-up of heat and humidity indoors: our little house has no air conditioning, other than leaving the windows wide open and hoping for a breeze.

I give up on styling my hair, which seems to resemble a bird's nest these days. It reacts very badly to humid conditions and I am wasting my time if I try to dry it with a hair dryer (not that I want to use it in these temperatures). Air drying results in loose curls, but these quickly frizz.

In the kitchen, I am battling the heat and humidity to make stock for the freezer. I am in the habit of saving chicken carcasses and dropping them in the freezer until I have the time to make stock. After a few busy months, there has been quite an accumulation of carcasses, to the point that Mr Candytuft is complaining. I have a marathon week of making chicken stock in the slow cooker, simmering down batch after batch and filling the freezer with the resulting chicken stock. It is worth the effort, though I could have chosen a cooler week in which to do this.

A walk on the boardwalk to escape the heat of the kitchen, allows me to notice that the colours of late summer are changing. There are lots of yellows and whites now, as the pinks of early summer have faded. The ospreys are still on the nest, but it can't be long now until they fledge, as their heads are clearly visible above the nest, as they start to explore the outside world. It is still very hot and humid, even in the early morning.

We drive out to visit the Green Park Shipbuilding Museum and Yeo House, passing through Grand River and the intriguingly named, Itch-a-Bit Drive (could it be that this is where all the mosquitoes and black fly live?). We pass the Roman Catholic church of St Patrick, which is a prominent landmark in the area. It was built in English Gothic style and is distinctive in yellow and white, with a tall central square entrance tower, which is topped by a central steeple.

Grand River was first populated in 1792, by Scottish immigrants from the islands of Barra and Uist, along with some from mainland Scotland. The original church was built of logs: the present church dates from 1836 but was enlarged and remodelled in 1890.

As we continue on our journey, the huge expanse of

Malpeque Bay stretches out before us. We pass an alpaca farm, where I spot some cria (baby alpacas) in the field with their mothers. We see field after field of potatoes, which are now in bloom, and corn, which is not quite as high as an elephant's eye, but is certainly growing in the summer heat.

When we arrive at Green Park Provincial Park, we decide to enjoy a picnic first before we browse around the museum. We seek shade and find a picnic bench under a tree, where we can sit and people-watch during our lunch. I packed a fresh baguette and some Boursin, which we enjoy before a small treat of chocolate cheesecake. It may not be the healthiest of lunches, but it certainly tastes delicious.

Green Park Shipbuilding Museum traces the origins of shipbuilding on Prince Edward Island, which was a major industry for most of the nineteenth century. In the age of sail, Great Britain needed timber and the vessels to carry it. Between 1800 and 1900, 4,500 vessels were built on Prince Edward Island. One of the great shipbuilding families of the era was the Yeos of Green Park.

James Yeo Snr was the son of a shoemaker and worked as a labourer until about 1814. He was unemployed, probably as a result of his drunkenness, and he immigrated to Prince Edward Island around 1819 because he faced starvation at home. He initially worked as a superintendent of the lumbering gangs but went on to become the richest and most influential man on Prince Edward Island, by the time of his death in 1867. He was a merchant, landowner and politician, but it was in shipbuilding that he made his fortune, building more than 340 vessels with his two sons, William James Jnr and John.

The shipbuilding boom collapsed in the 1870s as the days of tall ships and the sea captains who sailed them faded into history. The museum exhibits detail the trade routes of the ships, the sites of many shipwrecks off the shores of Prince Edward Island and feature many nautical items, including an original captain's log after a maiden voyage. The days of building tall ships may be long gone, but the heritage of the era lives on.

Yeo House was the home of the Yeo family. This elegant and historic home was built in the mid-nineteenth century by James Yeo Jnr. He was the son of James Yeo Sr, who founded the family fortune. This grand house was clearly the home of a very affluent family.

The exterior of the house is of yellow clapboard with green trim. It has three storeys and is topped by a cupola, which afforded James Yeo Jnr a fine view towards the harbour where his ships were being built. There is a tall central gable with an ornately decorative trim along the eaves and a large veranda, offering the family a shady place to sit out of the sun (though whether the ladies of the house ever sat on the veranda is unclear). The house is described as being of the colonial style and is certainly impressive. Even today, the proportions of the house would be described as generous.

Upon entering the house via the front door, we are met by the maidservant. She is dressed in the attire of the period: a full-length, plain light blue dress with long sleeves, over which she wears a white apron tied at the waist. She also wears a plain white cap over her hair. In real life, she is, of course, our guide and her job is to show us the home.

Touring this house is of more interest to me than viewing the museum, as I like to see the fashions and styles of the period and this grand house has plenty to offer. The ground floor is considered to be the public area of the house, where guests would be received in the formal parlour, or in the study if they were there on business. There is the formal parlour, complete with grand piano, where the children were strictly prohibited unless they were practising on the piano. Then there is the ladies' informal parlour, where they would work on their handicrafts and take afternoon tea at a round table, bedecked with a lace cloth. The young ladies of the household may have been allowed into this room to learn the social niceties of entertaining.

The walls of this room are decorated with a reproduction of

the original wallpaper, scraps of which were found after stripping back generations of wallpaper that had been added. The pattern is a soft gold with a floral design in apricot, yellow and white and is quite charming.

Moving on to the formal dining room, we find that the oval table, which seats six, is set for dinner. Upon the red tablecloth, there is the family's treasured Davenport china dinner service, which was brought all the way from England. The design is in pink and blue and this high-quality dinner service has stood the test of time and looks as good today as it must have looked when in regular use.

The backdrop to this grand table is the red and blue wallpaper: blue flowers on a slightly geometric pattern, which is highlighted in gold. In the far corner of the room, there is a serving hatch, where food, which was prepared in the kitchen, could be placed for the maid waiting at the table.

Moving on into the heart of the home and the area of interest to most visitors, we enter the kitchen. Three people ran this grand house: two maids and a hired man, whose job it was to ensure that the fires were continually burning in winter, as well as attending to the heavy work around the house and garden.

There is a huge hearth, where an open fire would have been used for cooking. The floor is uneven from years of back-breaking scrubbing by the maids, who actually wore the floorboards away down the knots in the wood: the knots being imperfections that cause living wood grain to grow around them, are harder and resistant to the constant scrubbing. A small central table is where they would take their meals. In the corner, there is a steep back staircase to the maids' bedroom (they shared one room). The hired man's quarters were separate and only accessible by a steep ladder at the back of the house. Underneath the main floor, there is a root cellar, where the provisions were stored for the winter.

In the study, there is a picture of a young Queen Victoria, hanging above the fireplace. The picture is from her coronation in 1838, when she was nineteen.

From the study, we return to the grand entrance hall with its elegant staircase, which leads up to the private rooms of the house. With a large family of ten children, James Jr needed a large amount of accommodation in which to house them all.

On this floor, there is the master bedroom with its grand furniture and discreet commode in the corner (the maids had to empty the commodes throughout the day, as the outhouse (privy) was at a distance from the house). The landing on this floor is covered by a hand-painted canvas mat in a geometric design in black and white, with a central floral motif.

The maids also had to assist the young ladies of the household to dress. On one bed, there is a day dress in burgundy and pink, together with a corset into which the maid would be required to lace the waist tightly to achieve the desirable 18 inches/45.5 cm. It is little wonder that there are fainting couches around the house as the ladies must have been passing out from an inability to breathe properly.

The boys of the household slept on the upper floor but had to move to the middle floor in winter, as it would have been too cold on the top floor. For safety reasons, there were no fires lit in the children's bedrooms.

We venture to the uppermost part of the house and into the octagonal cupola (without our guide), which necessitates a climb up a steep ladder (less than elegant, as I'm wearing a dress, but thankfully, there is no one else around!). I don't want to miss out on seeing the view, but we are disappointed. In the years since the Yeos lived in this house, the trees have matured and it is no longer possible to see the shore.

***

One morning finds us both up early, before dawn, as the heat and humidity prevent sleep. I make tea and watch the sunrise. Later, I harvest cucumbers from our garden and make dill pickles. I pick my first sweet peas of the season: they are late flowering due to our cold, wet spring and are disappointingly few, considering the number of seeds that were sown. I place the few that I collect in a small pink bud vase and enjoy their fragrance.

I head out to the orchard stand to buy vegetables for Sunday dinner. As I drive along the highway, I spot red lights flashing and think I am approaching an accident, but discover it is members of the local fire department who have set up two of their trucks in the middle of the road and are collecting tolls from passing drivers. It is a fundraiser for the local volunteer fire department and one of the firemen accepts my donation in a large boot. Naturally, I have to make a second contribution on my return trip, as they are collecting from both sides of the road. Still, it is all in aid of a good cause.

***

Summer is passing quickly and busy days working long hours have prevented me from going out for long walks recently. As I am now off for a couple of weeks and it is a beautiful morning, we head down to the boardwalk for fresh air and exercise. Mr Candytuft's ongoing knee problems have limited the time he spends walking, so I have lost my daily walking companion. He has found that riding his bike puts less strain on his knee, but he is determined to join me for a walk today.

It is mid-August, but there is a feeling of change in the air. The heat and humidity of recent weeks have gone, at least for the moment, to be replaced by a crisp feeling to the early morning air. It was actually so cool last night that I had to get up and close the window, which has been wide open for weeks, except at times of heavy rain. We have had several big storms with torrential rain, which have only added to the existing humidity.

Today is mild and sunny with a light breeze. The tide is out – low tide was about thirty minutes ago. The harbour is almost dry to a point about 250–300 metres/800-1,000 feet from the shore, where the water is little more than ankle-deep.

The colours of late summer are reflected in the plants. The white heads of cow parsley are turning to seed heads, which resemble birds' nests. Orange rose hips have appeared where there were flowers until quite recently, but the pale pink wild roses are still in bloom. I pause to inhale their perfume and watch bees buzzing around inside their open flower heads, becoming drunk on nectar.

There is a salty breeze, which is cooling and refreshing but even with the lower temperatures, the sun is hot in the more sheltered places along the shore. The red squirrels, which have been absent during the hot and humid days, have reappeared and are as cheeky as ever, running up to us in the hope of peanuts, but they are out of luck today. There is no sign of the ospreys now, so they must have fledged in the ten days since I was last down here. Mr Candytuft says he hasn't seen them for a week or more.

We are on our return trip when Mr Candytuft announces that his feet are hot and he intends to paddle all the way back to the car. I opt to continue on the boardwalk. I make faster progress, so decide to find a place to sit and wait for him along the shore, rather than in our hot car. I follow a grassy path towards lighthouse. I have seen people sitting down here, but have never done so myself.

I reach a bench and kick off my shoes. I can see Mr Candytuft in the distance and he is quite far offshore, but still in the shallows. I listen to the sounds of nature – the gulls calling and the winds whispering through the grasses and reeds along the shore. There is a small stream flowing onto the beach and it has attracted a group of gulls, which are enjoying a communal bath, as well as drinking from this source of fresh water.

The sun is pleasantly warm and I savour the fresh sea breeze blowing across the red sands. The view is of red sand with shallow patches of blue, where the tide has gone out. There is deeper water in the distance and a white lighthouse on the far shore. In the harbour, there is a lone sailboat tacking across – its white sail catching the wind and speeding its progress.

I enjoy being in the moment, with only the sounds of nature and my own thoughts for company. This is the perfect way to spend my free time.

***

I wake to the sound of the rain, which started sometime during the night. At first, it is fairly light but, as the morning progresses; it turns into a torrential downpour that persists for the rest of the day. I take advantage of the dismal weather and sit down to catch up on my writing. I listen to the rain on the roof and stare at the rain-smeared window. What little I can see of the sky over the roof-top of the neighbouring house looks heavily overcast and grey.

In need of comfort food on this autumnal day, I have a vegetable soup cooking in the slow cooker. I decide to make an apple crumble for dessert, which I will serve with custard. I use the remaining apples from last year's harvest (I found an extra bag at the bottom of the freezer).

At dusk, the rain is still falling. As the sun sets, it appears as a bright red ball on the western horizon, which sets fire to the sky. This comes as a surprise, as I stand and stare out of the kitchen window because we haven't seen a break in the cloud all day.

The rain stops during the night to be replaced by gusting winds, which are noisy enough to disturb my sleep. I get up during the night to close the window and eventually doze off again in a restless sleep.

***

It is Sunday morning and the sky is bright and sunny. I don't usually do laundry at the weekend, but we are running out of clothes, as the opportunities to dry laundry outdoors have been few and far between. I hang two loads on the line but they are only out for about an hour when black clouds roll in and it starts to rain. I run outside and stagger back in with a laundry basket full to overflowing with damp clothes. I hang them up to dry and the kitchen resembles Widow Twankey's Laundry, from the pantomime, *Aladdin*. Soon afterwards, the rain stops and the sun reappears, but I haven't the energy to play this game all day, so the clothes remain indoors.

A couple of days later I am listening to a song sparrow in our garden. He comes and sits on his favourite post and serenades me – well, I like to think he is singing to me, but I think he just loves life. Today, he stays on his perch long enough for me to get the binoculars out and take a closer look. Soon afterwards, something disturbs him and he flits off into a nearby tree.

A goldfinch appears and perches on the laundry line before visiting our bird bath for a drink. The goldfinches never stay long and this one is gone in a flash of yellow.

Earlier this morning, Mr Candytuft spotted a pair of crows perched on the edge of the bird bath. One of them was a fully grown fledgling, but still dependent on its parent for food. It was making lots of noise whilst the parent tore chunks from a piece of bread with its beak before dipping them into the water to soften them, then feeding the bread to its young. Quite where the bread came from, I have no idea, as we don't throw bread out for the birds.

Starlings are other frequent visitors to our garden and very noisy they are, too. They are often there in the early morning; pecking at the grass (I hope that they are eating the mosquitoes). The interesting thing to me is the fact that they ignore the bird bath, preferring to drink from a puddle that forms in our neighbour's garden. They also bathe in it: it puzzles me why they would choose to do so when there is a bird bath of fresh water close by.

Later, I return from a walk in the neighbourhood and spend

some time in the garden. Initially, I go out to harvest lettuce and tomatoes but get sidetracked into weeding the vegetable garden, thinning the strawberry plants (which are all leaves and no fruit) and transplanting a couple of plants to a bare patch in the front garden.

Despite my best efforts, three of my hollyhocks have died, including the large one we bought at the garden centre a few weeks ago. I am disappointed to lose it as it was supposed to flower this year. (Hollyhocks are biennials, so spend the first year growing a strong root system, then flower the following year.) The remaining four plants all started as tiny specimens but now stand almost knee-high, so appear to be thriving.

I have watched with envy as a neighbouring garden in the next street has burst into flower with hollyhocks in various shades of pink. They look so healthy and cheerfully bright with their distinctive spires of flowers standing tall next to the front door.

There is colour in the garden now – orange of calendula, white, purple and pink of various other plants out there, but the bed lacks any real height and is far from being the cottage garden of my dreams. Oh well, gardening requires patience and time – maybe next year.

My petunias have been a success and the two containers at the front of the house have been flowering for weeks. I go out and deadhead them and give them some water every couple of days and they favour me with yet more buds. I'm hopeful they will continue to bloom until the frosts arrive (which could be as early as mid-September).

The large sedum plants of the variety, 'Autumn Joy', are almost ready to put on their display of colour – the first hints of pink are now visible.

In the kitchen, we have been plagued by fruit flies for the last couple of weeks, even though I leave no fruit out and keep the tomatoes that I pick each day in a lidded container. I made a homemade trap of apple cider vinegar, a squirt of soap and a lid of plastic wrap with a few tiny holes punched in it and collected thirty to forty fruit flies in a week. I changed the vinegar this morning and collected another twenty in the course of a couple of hours and still, I see them buzzing around.

I bake Whitby lemon buns, which I had intended to bake at the beginning of the month. The first day of August is Yorkshire Day: with Yorkshire roots, it seemed appropriate that we should mark the occasion. It was, however, so hot and humid at the beginning of the month that I abandoned the idea and it has taken me three weeks to get around to making them.

It is a lengthy process mixing the dough, kneading it (for which I use my stand mixer) and then leaving it to prove for an hour and a half before dividing it into buns and leaving it to prove again, which takes a further hour.

The buns come out of the oven looking lightly browned and I ice them with lemon icing once they are cool. We enjoy them with a cup of tea – Yorkshire Gold, of course! They are delicious and well worth the effort.

During the summer months when everyone is busy with various activities, it can be hard to catch up with friends and loved ones, so it is a pleasure to catch up with my friend in Norway and chat for an hour across the miles. Like most of Europe, Norway has experienced a scorching summer this year and they are feeling the heat – not least because this weather is extremely unusual for them. The past week or so has seen an easing of temperatures on both sides of the Atlantic and it is with a sense of relief that I acknowledge the fact that summer is almost over.

I notice a change to the morning light with softness around the edges, which we only get as the season moves towards autumn. Technically, it may still be about a month away, but the seasons are not ruled by the calendar, particularly in this part of the world.

***

It is the weekend of the Atlantic Air Show, a biennial event that is expected to attract around 400,000 visitors, and Friday is the practice day. I'm out in the garden when the Snowbirds fly past in a formation. Their distinctive red CT-114 Tutor aircraft with their turbo-jet engines roar across the sky. This is the Royal Canadian Air Force's famous demonstration team.

This weekend will see demonstrations by the CF-188 Hornet team, also from the Royal Canadian Air Force, and the Canadian Army's Skyhawks' Parachute Team with their trademark Canadian Maple Leaf parachutes, as well as civilian performances of aerobatics.

Later in the afternoon, I hear the distinctive rotor noise of a helicopter, in this case, the CH-146 Griffon, which is a tactical transport helicopter, with its primary role being the transportation of troops and materiel.

The aircraft we see most often over our skies are the RCAF Hercules, which are frequent visitors to the Island. However, they are currently tasked to fight forest fires in British Columbia.

British Columbia may be the other side of the country but the forest fires have far-reaching effects. We are being affected by a large plume of smoke at high altitude, which leads Environment Canada to issue an air-quality statement today. As a result, our sky is hazy for much of the day and the sun has a reddish tinge.

I drive into town on Saturday morning and the queue of traffic travelling to the Air Show is lined up for a couple of kilometres. I think that coming out today was probably a bad idea, as it is going to take ages to get back home.

I am visiting the British food section of one of the supermarkets in town, in search of a small chocolate treat, when I meet two women who are looking at the various goodies on offer. I pick up a chocolate bar and one of them asks me if the chocolate is good. When I answer her question, she says, 'You aren't from the Island, are you?' I explain I am originally from the UK. She asks if these products are available there and I tell her that all of them are British.

We get into a conversation about British chocolate as compared to Canadian and chocolate from the US. By the time our conversation ends, I have convinced her to try Hobnobs biscuits and I tell her I should go before I convince them to buy half of the products on the shelf. This little corner is a bit of home and the only place in town where I can buy some of my British favourites.

I return home after visiting the library, where I'm fortunate to find I'm the first person to borrow a book that I read was a recommended read in *The Sunday Times*. I regularly trawl through their book recommendations and search for them on the library's website, in the hope of being able to borrow them. If they don't have the recommended books, it is possible to recommend a purchase and I have found that a couple of my suggestions have been acted upon.

Later, I'm out in the garden watering the vegetable patch and some of the container plants. The mosquitoes are out in force and I'm quite badly bitten by the time I return indoors, despite swatting at them in vain, attempting to dissuade them from eating me. Every time I get bitten, I react quite badly and end up with enormous, itchy lumps, which take more than a week to go down. It is little wonder I choose not to spend much time outside unless it is windy, in which case they seem unable to fly.

***

One expression that may be a little alien to British ears is to 'take a rain check'. For years, I never really understood the concept of this beyond postponing an event or invitation, but it has another meaning here, which I have only recently experienced.

Every week, we collect a pile of flyers from the same place where we pick up our mail and then we sit and browse through them. All of the larger retail establishments in town produce these and they show potential customers all of their products that are on sale at a reduced price for the coming week. I tend to confine myself to the grocery ones, as it is far too easy to spot something we didn't even know we needed until we see it at a special price. I only buy food that we would be buying anyway, although I will stock up on a couple of extras if the price is right.

One of the frustrations of this system is that everyone else has an eye for a bargain so, even if I am there at opening time on the day the sale starts, sometimes I am disappointed. For a long time, I accepted that a product was out of stock and thought no more about it until one day, I heard someone ask for a rain check. They were duly presented with a slip of paper.

After this, I tried the same thing myself and was given a rain check but, try as I might, every time I went back to the store to buy my favourite almond butter, it was still out of stock. Rain checks generally have expiry dates and I found my expired rain check in my wallet weeks later.

About a month ago, the same product was back on sale and I was there at the shop at opening time only to discover a gap on the shelf and no almond butter – again. I asked and the staff searched their warehouse, but they were unable to locate any. I got another rain check.

This morning, I went back as I realised that my rain check was about to expire tomorrow. My patience and persistence were rewarded: I found three jars of almond butter. I went to pay for them and told the cashier that I had a rain check, which I presented, and was duly given the products for half-price. I have finally been initiated into the use of a rain check!

***

I have long wished to visit the little community of Victoria, which is known locally as Victoria-by-the-Sea. This fishing village on the south shore of Prince Edward Island is a thriving community of artisans.

Located halfway between Summerside and Charlottetown, Victoria was founded in 1819 by the immigrant lawyer and agent for the Earl of Westmoreland, James Badin Palmer. His choice of location was based on the site being on the warmer waters of the Northumberland Strait and having a protected harbour.

By the end of the nineteenth century, Victoria was a thriving seaport: the third largest on the Island. Goods including potatoes, eggs and produce were shipped by sailing schooner, and later, visitors arrived by steamboat to enjoy a few days of rest and relaxation in this pretty village. Victoria became a quiet backwater once the Trans-Canada Highway arrived in the 1950s.

On the beautiful summer's afternoon of our visit, we arrive to find that the village is already busy with summer visitors. We manage to find a place to park close to the red and white Palmer's Range Lighthouse, which houses the Victoria Seaport Museum. The lighthouse stands adjacent to the shore and is of white clapboard with a red top. It is accessed via a boardwalk path from the road.

We stroll around the harbour and onto the dock, where children are enjoying the last days of their summer break – jumping into the warm waters of the harbour, before clambering back up the ladder onto the dock for another jump. One or two adults with them are demonstrating their diving skills but, for the most part, everyone is out to have fun.

The wharf includes a few shops and a pub, as well as the working part where the fishing boats are tied up – one or two of the fishermen are standing at the back of a pick-up truck chatting and sorting their gear.

We stroll around the end of the wharf where there is a patio area outside the pub. There is a tantalising aroma of fish and chips, as people enjoy their lunch.

At a craft/souvenir shop we are pleasantly surprised by the quality of the merchandise, which seems to all be produced locally or at least on Prince Edward Island. This is such a change from the usual junk on offer in many of the popular spots on the tourist trail.

As we are returning along the wharf, we see movement and a dark-coloured mammal crosses our path. It is smaller than an otter and at first I think it is a ferret. We start hunting around the cars parked on the dock to see where it went, along with other tourists who have spotted it. One of the fishermen tells me it is a mink, which comes to the wharf in search of fish. This is not a sight I expected to encounter today and is a first: I've never come across a mink before.

We walk along the road by the shore and pass a derelict property where nature seems to have taken over. We joke that this home is a 'fixer-upper' and Mr Candytuft goes as far as to suggest it may still be occupied, but it looks like it has long since been abandoned.

Heading up the main street on which most of the artisan shops are located, we pause to look in the pottery before continuing on our way. We admire the colourful houses and shops with pretty window displays to entice summer visitors to buy a keepsake to take home.

This community has a local population of 104 (2011 figure), but swells to accommodate the influx of summer visitors, many of whom are strolling around like us.

At the top of the street is The Orient Hotel, a century home which was established in 1900. This yellow clapboard building with white shutters and an enclosed porch area, which extends across the width of the building, is trimmed in blue. Today, it is run as a bed and breakfast.

I wonder about the many visitors who have stayed here in the last century and think about those first early tourists who arrived by steamship.

It is a hot afternoon and we find what shade we can, pausing to admire the famous Victoria Playhouse Theatre, which produces shows throughout the summer. We haven't managed to attend any yet – maybe this is a pleasure to reserve for next year.

Of all the shops we see, the Island Chocolate Shop towards

the bottom of the main street attracts the most attention. This cream clapboard building with green shutters draws visitors in for a closer look.

Entering the shop, we cross the wooden floor to the counter, where there is an old metal cash register with big buttons and a handle to wind at the side. The wooden shelves behind the counter are lined with teas, jars of honey and preserves, and there is a delightful aroma of chocolate and freshly ground and roasted coffee beans. We admire chocolate treats of all kinds: truffles and novelty items included.

The interior of the shop is cool as it is air-conditioned to prevent the chocolate melting. Through a window towards the back of the shop, we can see into the preparation area and watch the chocolates being poured, as everything is handmade.

In the centre of the shop, there is a chess set and chess board made entirely from chocolate. In this case, the opposing pieces are in milk and dark chocolate, as is the checker pattern of the board. I suppose if you are losing at chess, your opponent gets to eat your pieces!

We leave the cooling comfort of the chocolate shop and turn our steps towards the shore. Our visit to Victoria-by-the-Sea has been enjoyable and we have discovered a new place fairly close to home, where we can spend a pleasant afternoon.

It seems fitting that this is our final destination during August. There is a sense of an ending – the end of summer and the end of our year. A time for quiet reflection and a chance to wind down and relax in a more genteel place, away from the hustle and bustle of the more popular tourist areas.

EPILOGUE

ISLAND LIFE

A couple of weeks have passed and with them, the end of summer. The season is changing quickly as we reach the mid-point of September. The days are cooler and the night-time temperatures are hovering low enough for our first frost before the end of the month. There is a soft quality to the morning light that only occurs at this time of year, as the autumn equinox approaches.

In the garden, we are harvesting the fruits of our labours, with a glut of sweet, juicy vine tomatoes, delicious French beans, peas and mangetout. We have already harvested pickling cucumbers and lots of lettuce and beetroot.

As I write this, the starlings have finally found the bird bath, after ignoring it all summer and I interrupted five of them taking a bath yesterday morning. They were so funny, as they all leapt from the bath like blushing maidens and headed for a nearby wire, to dry out. They sat there looking all fluffy and ruffled. It was definitely a case of 'Who ruffled your feathers?'

Of course, I chose to start this account of my year in September because it felt like a time of new beginnings as well as endings.

When I look back at what brought us to this place, it has been a year of huge change. Maybe this is reflected in the fact that I was recently struck down by the worst dose of flu that I have had in years and I'm still coughing and congested two weeks later. Somehow, I can't seem to shake it off. Maybe this is my body's way of telling me I am taking on too much and I need to slow down and rest, to aid my recovery.

We have many things to be grateful for: we have food and shelter; a warm place to call home and we live in a very safe environment. Like many others, we came to Prince Edward Island for the quality of life and to get out of the rat race.

Housing is less expensive than in the city, but the wages are low and unequal to the cost of living, and the taxes are high. It has proven to be more expensive living here than we had initially thought it would be. There are also other expenses associated with living on an island, such as the exorbitant bridge toll to reach the mainland. To some degree, this can lead to feeling trapped and unable to afford to travel on a whim. Any trips to the mainland require careful planning and an extensive list so we don't forget something important. It isn't as if we can run back to Costco at the drop of a hat, as it is no longer a short drive, as it was when we lived in the city.

In contemplating a trip to the UK, I discovered that not only is it hugely expensive to travel from this part of the world, but it is lengthy due to the circuitous routes (Halifax-St John's, Newfoundland-Dublin-Manchester being one example). A trip back would take about twenty hours (minimum) and some journeys take more than a day: three flights on top of a three-hour drive to get to Halifax, Nova Scotia to catch a flight in the first place. This makes me realise how convenient and relatively inexpensive it was to fly from a major city, which offers direct flights, with no connections and lots of ticket options.

The winters are long and the summers are short. Anyone who visits Prince Edward Island as a summer visitor and enjoys glorious afternoons of seaside pleasures on the Island's famous red sand beaches has no idea what it is like to be in the same place in February. Many of the places that attract visitors during the season are closed for nine months of the year, including seasonal restaurants.

We have few visitors – people make vague promises to come and see us, but that is before they consider the twenty-three-hour drive to get here from Ontario, or the prohibitively expensive cost of domestic flights to Prince Edward Island.

We are looking forward to seeing some of our closest friends later in September when they pass through Charlottetown. They are taking a cruise and Charlottetown is one of their ports of call, so we will get to spend some time together, if only for a few hours.

It has been a year of exploration and discovery. On the whole, we have found the people of Prince Edward Island to be welcoming and friendly but, however long we live here, we will always be viewed as coming 'from away', which is the local term for people who were not born and bred here and without strong family connections to the Island.

There are many aspects to living here that we have found to be rewarding. There is a real sense of community, and with its low crime rate, it is a safe place to live. People have time for one another and are happy to chat and pass the time of day, even with strangers. They are genuinely interested in meeting us and finding out what brought us here. To some extent, I think they are surprised that we should choose to come and live on their island when we don't have local connections.

Although there is that sense of community here, we don't feel we have been fully absorbed into it. For me, I find it almost impossible to imagine living in one place all my life, but this is because I've experienced so many other places and cultures and I suppose this is what makes me accepting of the differences. We can't all be the same or have the same experiences, but we can all share the same values.

It is also a very peaceful place to live. At first, the silence at night was almost deafening to our city ears, which were accustomed to the noise associated with a city that never sleeps.

We had been accustomed to streetcars, trains, constant traffic, and aeroplanes overhead. Now, all we hear are the sounds of nature – mostly the crickets in the summer when the windows are open at night.

We have shared in national and local holidays and commemorations. We have worked and played here for a whole year now.

I don't know how long we are likely to be here and, with our track record, I wouldn't rule out another move. Personally, I don't feel the sense of permanence that those who were born here have – I have no deep roots or personal connections to this place. I still feel a yearning for home and family and a sense of connection that is missing. Being here on Prince Edward Island has restored a sense of balance to my life: I have learned to live in the moment. I have rediscovered that sense of joy, which I had lost in my former life.

As Mr Candytuft observed one day when he heard me singing along to the radio, 'I like to hear you sing because it means that you are happy.'

None of us knows what the future may bring but life is short, and we must make the most of it. For now, Prince Edward Island is the place we call home: our cradle on the waves.

ACKNOWLEDGEMENTS

It has been a joy writing this book about a year of our life together here on Prince Edward Island. At times I have struggled for inspiration, but that was mostly in the dark days of winter when I decided to take pleasure in ordinary everyday events. After all, we weren't here as tourists – we had moved here and were trying to get a feeling for Island life.

I would like to thank Paul for his support and encouragement in this project. Many thanks also go to Wendy Janes, my proofreader, for her painstaking review of my manuscript; to Tracy for reading some of my early chapters and to Terje for technical support.

ABOUT THE AUTHOR

Mae was brought up in England and trained as a nurse and midwife. She is a displaced Yorkshire lass, who relocated to Canada, living and working mainly in the big city before finding her way to the Maritimes. She currently lives on Prince Edward Island, where she enjoys walking, gardening, knitting, reading a variety of books and music.

Printed in Great Britain
by Amazon